£4.25+

Poor Relief
in
England and Wales
1601-1834

Geoffrey W. Oxley

Poor Relief
in
England and Wales
1601-1834

David & Charles
Newton Abbot London
North Pomfret (VT) Vancouver

ISBN 0 7153 6567 3
Library of Congress Catalog Card Number 74-81219

Set in 11 on 13pt Imprint and printed in Great Britain
by Latimer Trend & Company Ltd Plymouth
for David & Charles (Holdings) Limited
South Devon House Newton Abbot Devon

Published in the United States of America
by David & Charles Inc
North Pomfret Vermont 05053 USA

Published in Canada
by Douglas David & Charles Limited
3645 McKechnie Drive West Vancouver BC

For my mother and father

Contents

Introduction

Long before its abolition the old poor law had become the object of historical investigation. Among the better known of these early studies are Burn's sketch of 1764 and Eden's massive survey of 1797. They and others established the custom which required any serious contribution to the debate on poor relief to be prefaced by a suitable historical introduction. The report published by the Royal Commission on the Poor Law in 1834 was no exception to this rule and its historical interpretation of the system it was written to condemn, established what was to remain the orthodox view for many years. This view received its fullest expression in 1854 when Sir George Nicholls published his *History of the English Poor Law*. Updated with a minimum of revision in 1904 it remained the standard work well into the twentieth century. By this time, however, the old poor law was attracting the attention of historians with points of view very different from that of the Poor Law Commission. At one level the Hammonds and others were incorporating the poor law in the infant discipline of economic and social history and at another local historians were rediscovering the local records and using them to show what actually happened in particular places.[1]

The inter-war period saw a massive expansion of economic and social history. Poor law studies shared in this growth and saw the publication of three major works. The Webbs' *English Poor Law History* finally replaced Nicholls as the standard account and was usefully supported by Marshall's more popular description

9

of poor relief in the eighteenth century.[2] Meanwhile in the sphere
of local investigation Hampson's work on Cambridgeshire set a
standard which has rarely been equalled and never excelled.[3]
These works were symbolic of a major divergence of approach
to poor law history. On the one hand were those who addressed
themselves to the overall, national picture, relying heavily on
central sources;[4] on the other, local investigators concentrating
on their own parish, town, or county and the records created
therein.[5] Since the majority of those working at the national level
have been academics, and most, but by no means all, of those
working at the local level have been amateurs investigating their
own locality, differences of training and approach have tended to
exaggerate those already created by choice of subject and source
material. This divergence has been detrimental to the work of
both groups. Reading their publications, one cannot help feeling
that the national historians would have learned much from
familiarity with overseers' accounts and vestry minutes in addition to their knowledge of the pamphleteers' opinions on overseers and vestries, and that the local historians could have placed
their work in a surer perspective had they looked at the records
of neighbouring parishes to ascertain whether their own was
typical or unusual in the way it approached the problem of poor
relief.

This brings us to a criticism which can be levelled at both the
national and the local historians. Although they have produced
much valuable work during the last half century, few have made
full use of their predecessors' contributions to explain and il-
luminate their own. This is understandable. There is no satisfac-
tory bibliography of poor law publications, many of which take
the form of articles in local societies' transactions or chapters in
local histories which have virtually no circulation outside the area
to which they relate. The result has been that much of the work
on poor relief has been of the same type, for few researchers have
been in a position to develop the techniques and findings of their
predecessors.

It has only been in the last decade or so that we have seen a
significant attempt to remedy these two defects of reliance on a

limited range of sources and restricted knowledge of earlier findings. Recent years have seen the publication of much work which makes use of both national and local sources, building on the earlier work of others and seeking to test national generalisations against local evidence.[6] This is to be welcomed. We need a much more thorough investigation of administrative structures and relief methods before it will be possible to fit our findings in one particular parish into a clear and meaningful pattern.

Yet, in the final analysis, the investigation of poor relief in isolation is only foundation-laying. It can only be fully understood, and indeed make its fullest contribution to our understanding of the past, when it is seen in the wider context of the economic, social, political and other relationships of which it formed a part. Poor relief is part of the seamless web which constitutes the history of the human community in a particular locality. The historian of such a community must concern himself with many themes extending over a time span of two millenia or more. He cannot expect to acquire a specialised knowledge of all the evidence he will meet from prehistoric artefacts to computerised data in his local county hall but, if this knowledge is inadequate, his sources can so easily be misinterpreted or their potential not fully realised. It is for local historians, interested in all aspects of their community's past, that this book is intended. By describing the sources available to them and the sort of results which have been obtained from these sources in the past, it seeks to show how local historians can use the information available to them to explain the problems of poverty and the techniques of poor relief in the context both of the particular conditions prevailing in their community at any one time and of the general development of the relief system.

To achieve these ends it is necessary to bring together two components: an account of what was going on in the realm of poor relief between 1601 and 1834, and a description of the sources available to the researcher. The descriptive side has been investigated before and the Webbs treated it in greater detail and more comprehensively than will be attempted here. If their work is open to criticism, it is not that they missed any significant aspect of poor relief, but that on the information available to them they were quite unable to assess the relative significance of the various policies which they described. With the results of nearly fifty years' further research at our disposal it is possible to go farther down this road, although not as far as we may wish. We can, however, be more selective than were the Webbs; we can concentrate on those features which appear to have been commonest and thus erect a rudimentary framework into which the experience of any particular parish or locality can be fitted.

It is not possible to present this as a history of poor relief, for there is no such thing. There is only the history of poor relief in particular parishes. We do have totals for relief expenditure and so on for the whole of the country but they are of more significance for the impact they had on contemporaries than for what they tell us about poor relief, since they effectually hide the local differences which were the essence of the system. This does not mean there will be no place for narrative. When dealing with certain themes it is essential, but on the whole the approach must be thematic rather than chronological. The starting point therefore is the law by which the poor relief system was established and governed. This leads naturally to the other activities of the central government—enforcement, monitoring, the gathering of information—then to the activities of those who sought to influence the content of the law before it was made, or to describe it afterwards. From central government we shall progress to county government with its judicial and supervisory functions and so to the local parish or township where the actual work of relieving the poor was carried on. Having looked at its resources in men and money and the various ways they could be organised, we move to the crux of the problem—who were the poor, how can we identify the various forms of poverty and assess the problem facing a particular parish at a particular time? It is on the basis of our answers to these questions that we shall be able to judge the efficiency of the parochial administration and the relevance and effectiveness of the solutions it adopted. Our consideration of these solutions will begin with the simplest and commonest, ie pensions and occasional payments in cash and in kind. We shall then see how these simple forms of outdoor relief were expanded to deal with new problems, to exploit new facilities, such as the possibilities for medical relief, and to deal with the specialised problems presented by children. Next we shall consider what is perhaps the most significant innovation of the old poor law, institutional relief, tracing the origin and growth of the workhouse movement, examining its objectives and seeing how individual houses were organised in the pursuit of these. Finally we shall turn to the problem which beset all overseers of the poor, whether they used outdoor or indoor relief. This was the problem of the able-bodied which was a major factor in the establishment of the poor law, continually reappearing in both the agricultural and the industrial sectors and which finally, when it got out of hand in the form of what is generally called the Speenhamland System, brought about the demise of the old poor law.

Notes to the Introduction are on page 124

Chapter I
Policy and Supervision

Under the Act of 1601 three tiers of government were involved in the administration of poor relief. At the top were the central government, the crown, ministers, parliament and those seeking to influence their decisions and record their effects. The lowest tier was at parish level where the detailed work of raising money and distributing relief was carried on. Between the two stood the local magistrates whose duties were supervisory and included appointing officers, auditing accounts and settling disputes. In this chapter and the next we shall be looking in more detail at these three levels of administration to identify the precise part played by each and the way its activities can be reconstructed from the records which have come down to us.

Legislation

The primary function of the central authorities was the enactment of the legislation by which the poor law was established and subsequently altered, amended and improved. It is unnecessary to look in detail at the mass of legislation produced in the two centuries or so after 1601. This has already been done elsewhere[1] and the acts themselves are readily available in the *Statutes at Large*. They can easily be found with the aid of the lists printed by Eden and the Webbs.[2] Here we need only indicate the main landmarks of legislative history and leave detailed discussion of

14

particular enactments until we are considering the matters to which they refer.

Compulsory, rate-financed poor relief, which was the essence of the poor law, was first established by an Act of 1597,[3] re-enacted in a revised form in 1601.[4] This legislation was the culmination of half a century of evolution and experiment. The details do not concern us here but a little of the background is necessary for an understanding of the form and content of the Act which governed poor relief down to 1834. The sixteenth century did not discover poverty but found it taking new forms and appearing on a much greater scale than before. Behind this lay the well-known economic and social changes which the country experienced during the century: conversion to pasture, the great inflation, changes in overseas trade routes, the development of new industries and the transformation of old ones, rising population and so on. Two types of poverty became especially noticeable towards the end of the century. In certain towns where the textile industries had attracted large numbers of artisans the problem was the mass destitution which such people suffered whenever the industry employing them encountered a depression. This presented a serious problem to the urban authorities whose responsibilities included both the preservation of law and order and the prevention of mass starvation. In rural areas the problem was less concentrated but no more tractable. It concerned people made unemployed by the combined pressures of agricultural changes and rising population. The only resort for the unemployed farm labourer was to take to the road in search of work. If none was forthcoming it was all too easy to slide into vagrancy, mendicancy and crime, and to join with others in the same situation to form a band of sturdy beggars able to terrorise those on whom they preyed.

Thus the problem of poverty became an integral part of the problem of law and order, the maintenance of which was essential to the continuance of effective government. Official policy towards poverty was therefore determined by policy towards law and order. The central aim of this policy was the suppression of vagrancy and the begging that went with it. It was all very well to punish those convicted of these offences but little was achieved if nothing was done about those who were too old or sick to live by working and relied on alms, or those who were genuinely travelling in search of work. Since the relief of the deserving poor was seen primarily as a task for charity, legislation was passed to encourage organised charity and the establishment of endowments to support almshouses, supply doles to the poor and pay for the apprenticeship and training of workers. But what if these sources were inadequate? This was where the poor law came in, as a safety net to catch those who were not liable to conviction as vagrants but for whom available charitable resources were inadequate. It envisaged two main activities. The first was setting the able-bodied poor to work whether they be children whose parents could not support them, youths who could be trained by means of an apprenticeship, or adults to be supplied with materials on which they could work. Secondly, arrangements were to be made for all those old, sick and disabled who could not support themselves. All this was to be financed by a compulsory rate levy in place of the often more or less compulsory charitable donations of earlier acts.

In this way it was recognised that the changes which had created or aggravated these problems had also created the resources needed to deal with them. The creation of a sound financial base was of great significance. The act was intended to fill the gaps in a social policy designed with sixteenth-century conditions in mind, but it was worded so vaguely that it could be adapted as conditions changed to meet the needs and problems of very different periods. The history of the poor law down to 1834 is essentially the history of how these imprecise duties and sound financial base were exploited with varying degrees of success to meet the problem of poverty in all its varied manifestations.[5]

There was however, a more immediate problem. Legislation in the statute book had to be transformed into action in the localities. One of the reasons why there were so many poor law enactments during the sixteenth century was the difficulty of securing their enforcement. Eventually much repetition combined with the inescapable pressures of the problem itself to compel action, and there is ample evidence that the laws were being enforced in many of the towns and villages of southern and eastern England by the 1590s. There have been a number of useful studies of how the rudimentary poor law was implemented around the turn of the century and it is reasonable to assume that the few parishes from which records have survived were fairly typical of their localities.[6] Less work has been done on the local operation of the poor law in the first half of the seventeenth century, but later evidence indicates that ground which had been gained was rarely lost if only because the continuing presence of recipients made it impossible to terminate a relief system once it had been inaugurated. Indeed, it is probable that more parishes were introducing relief systems.[7] This period of implementation reached its climax during the 1630s, when Charles I made proper provision for the poor one of the objectives of his personal rule. His privy council issued directives to local magistrates and instructed them to report on what was being done. As a result we can see not only that the poor law was being enforced but how it was being enforced.[8] The magistrates' returns not only show the extent of poor relief in this period but give much information about how different local authorities were going about their task. It is clear that by the outbreak of the Civil War rate-financed poor relief extended to all but the remotest parts of England and Wales—some parts of the principality had to wait another half century or more before either the needs of the poor demanded, or the level of prosperity permitted, poor rates to be levied.[9]

There has been some dispute about the effects of the Civil War on poor relief. Naturally the removal of constant pressure from the privy council gave all concerned an opportunity to slacken their efforts and the confusion of warfare must have disrupted orderly administration in many areas. But the poor did not disappear. In some places their numbers may even have been swollen by disabled soldiers and by people deprived of their livelihood through dislocation of war. The continuing pressure of the problem was enough to ensure that poor relief was not discontinued. In most places the question is unlikely to have arisen. It is true that some outlying areas had no system of poor relief before the

B

1630s, but elsewhere the collection of money and its distribution among the poor had gone on for up to two or three generations. It was hardly likely that such a well-established custom would collapse easily and the evidence confirms that it did not. Few overseers' accounts have come down to us from this period but those we do have show clearly the way in which the payment of pensions continued unabated during the war.[10] Relief of the poor did not wither away at the first cold blast.[11]

The breakdown of Charles I's personal rule did not signal a cessation of poor relief but it was nevertheless a watershed in poor law history. It marked the end, as far as the old poor law was concerned, of government efforts to secure the enforcement of the law. From now onwards it was assumed, quite rightly, that the law was being put into effect and the energies of the central authorities were directed towards other ends. This change is, perhaps, of greater significance to historians than it was to the poor because it heralds a major shift in the type of sources which can be used. We owe our detailed picture of the way in which poor relief was organised in the 1630s to the reports gathered by the privy council. The few overseers accounts which have survived serve to fill out the details and push the story back in time. From 1640 to 1700 we are dependent entirely on overseers' accounts and other local records, of which there are very few for this period. We know the poor law was in operation after the Restoration, but we know less about it then than we do about poor relief in the 1630s. Although after the Civil War the central government withdrew from its role of enforcement, it was still active in the enactment of legislation. In fact the last four decades of the seventeenth century were exceptionally fruitful in this respect.

The most important matter dealt with was a problem which arose naturally out of the original decision to make each parish responsible for the relief of its own poor. There was much to be said for making each socio-economic community responsible for the relief of its own destitute and unemployed but while each such community as a whole had a continuing existence, people could, and did, move from one place to another. Thus arose the question of which parish was responsible for the man who had moved around a few times during his life—his birthplace, the place where he had lived longest, the last place where he had lived a specified length of time, the place where he became destitute? This uncertainty put parish authorities in a dilemma. If a newcomer arrived, were they to expel him lest he became chargeable or allow him to come because there was an employment vacancy which he could fill? The same dilemma afflicted those concerned with national policy. Was there any sense in supporting a man out of public funds in one place when there was work in another? If he went, did there come a point when the new parish where he was spending his labour became responsible for his maintenance in sickness and old age, or was he to be returned in his declining years, as a virtual stranger, to the place he left as a youth? No doubt considerations of convenience and comfort weighed least with those devising the legislation, but even so the problem was complex enough. How could they permit mobility of labour and allow people to become settled where they had made their contribution to the economy without rendering the parish liable for the relief of every casual visitor or passenger?

The first legislation for settlement was in 1662.[12] It is clear from the preamble to the act that it was enacted under pressure from parishes needing stronger powers to rid themselves of unwanted and potentially chargeable immigrants. It legalised removal, laying down a formal procedure and specifying that it must take place within forty days of arrival. Hedged about as it subsequently was with qualifications and exceptions, forty days' residence remained the basic qualification for gaining a settlement. The act itself contained some exceptions. Persons renting a tenement worth £10 a year or more, and those who could give the parish security for its indemnity should they become chargeable, were exempt from removal. It also made an interesting provision for people travelling for temporary or seasonable employment such as harvest work. They were to carry with them a certificate from their parish officers agreeing to take them back.

Experience showed that these rules were too heavily weighted in favour of the immigrant. In the towns where the problem was most serious it was all too easy to remain for forty days without the knowledge of the authorities. Accordingly an Act of 1685[13] decreed that the forty days should run from the day written notice was given to the overseers and an Act of 1691[14] that the notice should be read out in church and entered in the overseer's account book. This legislation firmly tilted the balance the other way but, to compensate, the 1691 Act added to the list of circumstances in which a settlement might be gained without giving notice: service for a year in an annual public office, paying public taxes, and remaining irremovable by virtue of being bound apprentice to a master resident in a particular place. In 1697[15] this principle was extended to unmarried persons hired to serve for a year as servants. This act also made some important changes in the law regarding certificates. They were now extended to cover permanent movements but, to be valid, had to be issued by the overseers and churchwardens, attested by two witnesses and approved by two magistrates.

Thus, over a period of forty years, a legal framework was evolved which achieved most if not all the objectives required of it. It gave parishes power to remove those actually or potentially chargeable, while making it unnecessary in the latter case if a certificate was brought showing whither the bearer was to be removed when the need arose. The law facilitated removal by the parish and movement by the population, but it restricted the opportunities for people to gain a legal settlement where they were physically settled. In practice only the better off who could rent a £10 tenement, pay taxes, or serve an office, and the young over whose servitude or apprenticeship the parish had no control, could change their settlement easily.

The only major amendment to this structure before 1834 was in 1795[16] when parliament generalised two practices which were already normal in some areas. The first gave everyone the status of certificatemen by decreeing that nobody might be removed until actually chargeable; the second prevented the forcible removal of those unfit to travel—in the very nature of things a frequent occurrence—by making provision for the place of settlement to pay relief granted in the meantime by the parish of residence. These changes tended to humanise the operation of the settlement laws but they did not alter their basic content. Other developments in the rules of settlement during this period are to be found, not in the statute books, but in the law reports. No aspect of the poor law produced so much litigation as did the settlement laws. A glance at the relevant section of a volume such as Burn's *Justice* or some similar work[17] will reveal the host of obscure situations and perverse technicalities which the courts had to examine before they could determine points of dispute. For the most part the matters raised are of no general significance and the lawyers' careful description of them can blind one to the smoothness and efficiency with which the law was generally put into operation.

Settlement was not the only poor law matter which gained the attention of late seventeenth-century legislators. The same Act of 1662[18] which introduced the principal of removal also contained the important provision that, where a parish was exceptionally large, each township within it should be responsible for its own poor. As with settlement this was a matter of tidying up a loose end left by the 1601 Act, and its implications will be looked at more fully when we come to examine the position of the parish as a unit of local government. The 1690s saw the enactment of several important statutes besides those dealing with settlement. They were years of high food prices and severe pressure on the rates. The government responded with investigations by the Board of Trade—the first, and least successful, attempt to gather information about relief expenditure in every parish—and a legislative programme designed to tighten up efficiency and cut the costs of relief.[19] The settlement laws fitted into this scheme along with provisions that the poor should indicate their state by wearing badges and provisions for the limitation of, and if possible contraction of, parish pension lists.[20]

This decade also saw an important new departure in poor law legislation. By the 1690s many towns had been operating poor relief schemes for a century or more and they were coming to realise that the powers granted in the general legislation had not

always given them the constitutional strength or the legal
authority to organise relief as efficiently as they wished. The
device used to overcome these problems was the local act of
parliament. Legislation had been used in connection with the
London Corporation of the Poor earlier in the century[21] but its
regular use by poor law authorities was initiated by Bristol in
1696.[22] Other towns, mostly in the west of England or on the
east coast, soon followed suit. There were seven such local acts
passed in the next year and another five in the following fifteen
years, in addition to two acts amending those passed in the initial
rush as well as several unsuccessful applications to parliament.
We are not concerned here with the detailed provisions of these
acts[23] but with the significant change in the role of the central
authorities which they represent. In the sixteenth and early
seventeenth centuries it had been the task of government to
stimulate local action for the relief of the poor, first through
legislation and later through administrative action. Now the
boot was on the other foot. The localities were doing the job and
finding it necessary to come to the central authorities asking for
the powers they needed to do it better.

After the first flush of enthusiasm for local acts there was something of a lull until the middle of the eighteenth century. A few
new parishes or groups of parishes obtained local acts for the
first time but there was more activity from those which already
had them seeking amendment acts. This decline in interest may
be explained in part by the fact that in 1722 parliament made the
powers for the establishment of workhouses usually contained
in local acts available to all parishes.[24] It was not until 1749 that
there was a marked renewal of interest in local acts. This revival
was led by parishes in the suburbs of London which often included provisions for poor relief in acts also dealing with lighting,
watching and other aspects of local government relevant to this
area of rapid urbanisation. Enthusiasm for local acts was not
confined to the London area but extended to towns in all parts
of the country, nor did it die away after a short period. From
now onwards hardly a year went by without parliament passing
at least one local poor law act.

Copies of these acts are rarely to be found outside the localities to which they relate but there is a convenient list of those passed before 1797 in Eden's *State of the Poor*, pp ccxl–cclxxvii, and those from before 1801 are to be found in the *Chronological Table of Statutes* (HMSO annual editions from 1960). Later local acts are to be found in the *Index to Local and Personal Acts*, 1801–1947 (HMSO, 1949), pp 386–584. There they are listed with other local government acts under the places to which they relate, arranged in alphabetical order.

Among the local acts one group is worth singling out for special mention because it represents an almost unique attempt to spread to rural areas the advantages which, for nearly a century, the towns had been deriving from legislation made to meet their own particular needs. There were eight such acts. The first was passed in 1756, the remainder between 1763 and 1765. Each gave these special powers to one or a pair of the ancient hundreds in Norfolk or Suffolk.[25] Eventually thirteen hundreds were thus included in incorporation. This movement did not spread further, but twenty years later in 1782 Gilbert's Act was passed in an attempt to make available to all the advantages enjoyed by local act districts.[26] It was a permissive act, setting out in detail the powers of union and workhouse organisation which were a common feature of the local acts in this period.

Though its attention was concentrated on local acts, parliament did not entirely neglect the general poor law legislation during the eighteenth century. Mention has already been made of the acts of 1722 and 1782 dealing with the union of parishes and the establishment of workhouses. They were the most significant of a series of acts, most of which were concerned with matters of detail, tidying and tightening up the existing legislation. As the century drew to a close, parliament once again turned its attention to matters of substance. Besides the first major change in the settlement laws for nearly a century the 1790s saw an important amendment of the 1722 Workhouse Act,[27] and legislation for the closer control of, and the prevention of abuse in, the pauper apprenticeship system.[28] The second decade of the new century saw major alterations to the parochial administrative structure through legislation, permitting the election of standing committees[29] and the appointment of paid officers.[30] These salient features of parliament's renewed interest in the poor laws are sufficient to indicate how the wheel had come full circle. Once again the central authorities were taking an interest in the general poor law. Even if the lead was being taken by back benchers rather than by the government, the ground was being steadily prepared for the more drastic and far-reaching reforms of 1834. The expansion of general legislation did not stem the flow of local enactments but it did emphasise the anomaly that allowed a minority of parishes to operate under specially beneficial terms to the detriment of the remainder and this added further strength to the movement for general reform.

Official Investigation

Momentum was also given to this movement by the mass of information about local poor relief administration which the central authorities had been gathering with increasing frequency during the half century before 1834. There had been earlier attempts to do so. In the 1690s returns of parochial expenditure had been obtained from incumbents through the ecclesiastical authorities, but the record of the results is incomplete and so arranged as to give no useful local information.[31] It was not until 1748 that parliament authorised the collection of similar returns. These were not printed at the time and their existence was forgotten until they were rediscovered and published in 1821.[32]

It was another twenty-five years before parliament resumed its inquiries unto the operation of the poor laws in the country at large. The years 1775-8 saw a series of select committees appointed to investigate various aspects of poor relief and vagrancy. Besides making numerous recommendations in their several reports and gathering a good deal of information from selected parishes they obtained returns on the cost of supporting and employing the poor in every parish. This was the first of four such major inquiries. It dealt with the financial year of 1775-6[33]

and its successors with 1783–5,[34] 1803[35] and 1813–15[36] respectively. Making comparisons between these years is obstructed by
the fact that the questions asked were slightly different on each
occasion but some compensation can be derived from the fact that
they became steadily more wide ranging. Full details of the information gathered in each of these years—and indeed on the
contents of all parliamentary investigations before 1835—are to
be found in *Hansard's Catalogue and Breviate of Parliamentary
Papers, 1696–1834* edited by P. and G. Ford. These four sets of
returns contain a vast quantity of information on the cost and
related aspects of relief, and as such constitute an indispensable
tool for the student of poor relief. The information on expenditure can be supplemented by information obtained in subsequent
years to give totals for every parish in every year from 1813 to
1830. Some of these returns also give information about the
spread of select vestries and assistant overseers and the number
of removals and appeals.

One effect of these inquiries was to bring home most forcefully to parliamentarians the rate at which relief expenditure was
rising. Their response was further investigation in search of
remedies. From 1813 onwards hardly a year passed without
either the Lords or the Commons appointing a committee to
investigate some aspect of poor relief. Their reports are of greatest
interest to those concerned with the evolution of poor relief
theory but the voluminous minutes of evidence which accompanied them provide an unrivalled source of detailed information and comment for those interested in the areas from which
the witnesses came. The period also saw the publication of
reports on many peripheral matters: education and charities,
conditions in agriculture and industry, emigration, the treatment of lunatics and crime. All these throw light on aspects of
poor relief and on developments in particular localities. These
reports and returns are not widely available although the large-
scale reprinting now being undertaken by the Irish University
Press is making at least some of this invaluable material available
in local libraries.

The culmination of this growing output of returns, reports,

and minutes of evidence was the Royal Commission which produced a report and six appendices in 1834.[37] The report itself is
naturally very generalised and chiefly concerned with the abuses
which the commissioners' inquiries had revealed and with their
proposed remedies. For anyone interested in how the problem
of poverty was being tackled in a particular locality or in the
more general problem of the distribution of particular policies
and practices the appendices will be the main focus of interest.
The commission appointed assistant commissioners to visit and
report on all parts of the country. Their reports are printed in
Appendix A, consisting of an indexed first part of over 900 pages,
and un-indexed second and third parts of about 250 and 200
pages respectively. The reports submitted by the assistants vary
greatly in length, content and quality. At one extreme D. O. P.
Okeden deals with Oxfordshire and Wiltshire in ten pages; at the
other Captain Chapman devotes 105 pages to Somerset, Cornwall, South Devon and portions of Wiltshire and Gloucestershire. On the whole the assistant commissioners were reasonably
thorough and their reports give a fair picture of the way poor
relief was organised in all parts of the country. In some cases the
reports have to be read with caution because their authors were
committed to a particular point of view and tended to write as
if arguing a case rather than presenting a factual report. Besides
arranging these personal investigations the commission sought
local information in the traditional way by asking for returns
from parish officers. The approach was different from earlier inquiries in that they asked many more questions but only sent
their questionnaire to a fraction of the total number of parishes.
There were two series of questions; one, addressed to rural
parishes, contained forty-five queries, some of which were revised
after the first returns had shown up the inadequacies of the earlier
versions. The urban parishes had to answer sixty-four questions.
The replies given by about 1,200 rural and 400 town parishes, or
in a few cases districts, hundreds or incorporations were set out
in full in Appendix B. They give a great deal of detailed information about the organisation of poor relief and the conditions of
the poor generally in the selected parishes and can be used to fill

out the general picture of particular regions presented by the assistant commissioners. This appendix has to be read in conjunction with Appendix C in which, under the heading 'Miscellaneous Communications' are printed any answers to the queries which were too long for inclusion within the rigid format of Appendix B. This appendix also contains several other communications submitted to the commission on various aspects of British poor relief. Similar reports from all parts of Europe and America are printed in Appendix F. Appendices D and E are concerned with more specialised matters. The latter deals with the peripheral question of vagrancy and the former with one aspect of the Speenhamland System—the labour rate. It contains reports on the way this had been operated in 142 parishes in nineteen southern and eastern counties, and again is a useful source of information about those particular places.

These appendices represented the largest accumulation of information about poor relief that had ever been made but they suffered from one obvious defect compared with previous inquiries: no attempt was made to gather even a limited quantity of information from every parish in a way which would bear comparison with the classic returns of 1776, 1786, 1803 and 1813–15. This fact alone laid the commissioners open to the criticism to which they have been subjected both by their contemporaries and subsequent investigators: that they approached the problem with preconceived ideas and that having selected their evidence on a partial basis they analysed it in an unstatistical and prejudiced manner. Much of this criticism is valid and it serves to warn the modern student against swallowing the report whole. The commissioners were concerned to promote change and a particular change at that. To do so they had to indict the existing system, to demonstrate the unquestionable necessity for change and then present an analysis of its faults which led directly to the corrective measures they wished to propose. But even when all this has been said it does not detract from the enormous value of the appendices to the inquirer seeking to understand the operation of the poor law in a particular locality. Of course some of the assistant commissioners had the same

preconceptions as their masters and this must be allowed for
when sifting their facts from their opinions and analysing their
choice of facts. Even the parish officers who answered the ques-
tionnaires had their pet theories but they were much more varied
and it is quite simple to distinguish the answers giving fact from
those giving opinion. The commissioners may have ignored evidence unfavourable to their preconceptions but they did not
suppress it and the result is that the last few years of the old
poor law are far more fully documented than any other period in
its history.

Commentary, Criticism and Analysis

While the government and the parliamentarians were busy with
the tasks of legislation and inquiry their work was subjected to a
continuous barrage of comment and criticism from those with
ideas to propagate, schemes to promote, and axes to grind. The
field of theory and propaganda was not entirely divorced from
that of practical activity. Thus Thomas Gilbert,[38] who made
much use of the printed word and was the prime mover behind
several parliamentary inquiries, had more success than most
members in pushing poor law legislation through parliament, and
Richard Burn[39] was the author not only of an often quoted pamphlet but also of one of the best-known legal treatises, besides
being an active magistrate in Cumberland. Even so, for the
student of poor law history, the polemical literature is signifi-
cantly different from the other sources he encounters. Normally
he is dealing with dry, factual and often routine administrative
records. Sometimes legislation may express hopes beyond a
government's powers of achievement, or minutes intentions that
were never fulfilled, but the hopes and the intentions were
genuine enough and in marked contrast to the world of specula-
tion, hypothesis and controversy which is met in the pamphlets.
The most useful bibliographies of these publications are L. W.
Hanson, *Contemporary Sources for British and Irish History,
1701–1750* (Cambridge 1963) and Henry Higgs, *Bibliography of*

Economics 1751–1775 (Cambridge 1935), while several writers have compiled bibliographies of particular periods or themes and summarised the contents of many of the publications they list.[40] On the whole the writings of the propagandists are not of great interest to those concerned with what actually happened in the parishes. Generally their first concern was with schemes for the future. Present conditions were only referred to in order to justify the change and then in the form of generalisations too sweeping to be of value, or unsubstantiated assertions which must be checked against other evidence before they can be relied upon.[41] This is not to say that contemporary writers never published reliable and useful factual information on poor relief and allied topics. A minority undoubtedly did. The two editions of an anonymous pamphlet entitled *An Account of Several Workhouses*[42] were certainly printed in order to recommend this type of relief, but they did it by recording invaluable factual information about more than one hundred institutions in operation within ten years of the first general workhouse act being passed. Even more information was gathered by Eden for his monumental work published in 1797. Besides summarising the statutes and pamphlet literature in a lengthy history of the poor law, he visited parishes in all parts of the country to investigate their methods of dealing with the problem of poverty. In his choice of parishes he showed a bias towards those which were larger and more populous and had relatively sophisticated but untypical organisations. Wherever he went he gathered information from parish records, conversations with officers and personal observation to produce a vast dossier on the organisation of relief in 1794–6.

Besides these general surveys numerous pamphlets were produced to describe or influence poor relief policy in particular localities. Many of them have survived only in a few copies, are not to be found in the general bibliographies and can often only be seen in the library serving the locality to which they relate. This is where they will be of greatest value because, when due allowance has been made for the bias of their authors, they can throw much light on local poor relief methods.

This kind of bias is the last thing one would expect from writers of the second major group of publications about the poor law. These are the legal treatises written from the early seventeenth century onwards in ever increasing numbers and bulk. They were intended to guide overseers and magistrates in the performance of their duties and one occasionally meets entries in minutes or accounts showing that parochial authorities did make use of this facility. Details of all these publications are given in Sweet and Maxwell's *Bibliography*[43] and, although the quality varies, these works can be very useful in giving a clear statement of how the law stood and was understood at a particular point in time. To do so, they inevitably had to summarise the decided cases, many of which concerned circumstances which were peculiar to say the least. Reading this catalogue of oddities can very easily give one a false impression of the poor law. Contrary to the impression given by the law books it was not concerned only about people with curious life histories, nor was it staffed only by persons devoted to the pursuit of profitless litigation.

The County Administration[44]

Between the central authorities with their policy-forming functions and the parochial officers who actually distributed relief, stood the county and borough magistrates whose task was to supervise the administration of relief in their areas, to see that the law was put into operation and to settle disputes. Acting alone, in pairs or in petty or full quarter sessions according to the magnitude of the issue their influence was felt at every point in the relief system. They appointed overseers and select vestries, audited accounts, issued or approved the documents needed in connection with settlement, affiliation and apprenticeship. They were also responsible for the settlement of disputes, the majority of which were either from those denied relief by the overseers, or more frequently in connection with settlement.

Apart from their signatures on the relevant documents we have very little record of how magistrates used their powers of

supervision and appeal jurisdiction outside quarter sessions, but
the records of this court provide a full account of what they did
as a corporate body. The survival rate of these records has been
excellent though they do not extend back to the start of our
period in every county. In addition a considerable amount of
quarter sessions material has been made available in print, in
calendar, extract or other form. The way in which the records
were kept varies from county to county and from period to period
but in the main there are three classes of document which will be
of interest to the student of poor relief: the main record of the
court, usually known as an order book or minute book (some
counties have both); the bundle of administrative papers which
support the main record and various documents which had to be
deposited or registered at the court.

The first two may be considered together as being part and
parcel of the same judicial and administrative function. They are
especially valuable for the seventeenth century when parochial
records are at their most sparse and when, by coincidence, the
sort of business coming before the courts was most interesting.
This is because when the relief system was first being established
the magistrates were obliged to interfere in the details of management to ensure that the law was enforced. This was especially
true during the period of Privy Council during the 1630s. The
novelty of poor relief also meant that many more poor people
had to appeal to quarter sessions before they could obtain relief.
Consequently where the records have survived we have a detailed
picture of the machinery and functions of early relief administration.[45] Once it had become firmly established the machine ran
according to custom and requests for relief were dealt with
locally in accordance with precedent and these matters were
rarely aired at quarter sessions. The result is that most eighteenth-
century sessions records are chiefly concerned with settlement
appeals, affiliation matters and other routine business, and it is
only occasionally that a case shedding useful light on parochial
relief administration appears. Some of these exceptions were very
important, however. The notorious Speenhamland Scale was
produced during one of the Berkshire magistrates' rare forays

into the field of relief administration and records of other similar interventions are to be found elsewhere, earlier, and then with growing frequency in the following decades.[46]

The nature and usefulness of documents deposited with quarter sessions varies greatly from county to county. Among the more valuable items which may be found are foundation agreements for Gilbert Unions and the original parochial returns made in connection with parliamentary inquiries. Equally useful are some of the county records not themselves concerned with poor relief: land tax returns provide a comprehensive record of parish officers; enclosure, tithe and other maps can be a reliable aid to the location of workhouse buildings. County records were concerned with so many aspects of local life that there are few problems the poor law student will meet that cannot be at least partially elucidated from them.

Retrospect from the New Poor Law

The records of the higher levels of government did not become silent on the workings of the old poor law as soon as it was replaced by the new. It was several years before unions took over from parishes in all parts of the country and during the transition period the records are full of information about the situation which the boards of guardians found and their problems in implementing the changeover. Parliamentary inquiries continued. A voluminous quantity of evidence was taken by the select committees of 1837–8 and there were also investigations of particular problems, such as the Gilbert Unions which remained outside the new system, and of conditions in particular places. The main reports are listed in P. Ford and G. Ford, *Select List of British Parliamentary Papers, 1833–1899*, and some of them have been reprinted in the IUP series.

A similar concern with the past is also to be found in the early reports and records of the new administration established under the Poor Law Amendment Act. The early reports of the Poor Law Commissioners appointed to supervise its implementation are chiefly a record of their formation of unions and the situations and obstacles which confronted them while doing so. The information to be found in these reports can be supplemented from the archives of the commissioners. These are held at the Public Record Office among the records of the Ministry of Health. The most useful classes are MH 12, correspondence with individual unions and MH 15, indexes to this correspondence. The letters for each union are filed together and a full list of all the available material is being published by the List and Index Society.[47] The commissioners' records also contain files of their circulars, correspondence with assistant commissioners and authorisation of expenditure on workhouse extention or construction. In all these cases the early items contain material looking back to the previous system. At the local level parishes were grouped into unions and the administration of poor relief was transferred to boards of guardians. Their early minutes should never be neglected by the student of the old poor law. Some contain detailed accounts of all the paupers in their area, others reports on workhouses and other specialised services, although not a few manage to be quite silent about the system they superceded.

In the field of poor relief, therefore, it was the function of the central government to create a legal framework and of the county government to enforce the law and adjudicate disputes. In so doing they created extensive records which can be of immense value to the historian but the real decisions were taken and the work of relieving the poor actually performed at the parochial level, so it is to the administrative machinery and records created at this level that we must now turn our attention.

Notes to this chapter are on pages 124–6

Chapter 2

The Parochial Executive

The Unit of Administration

The Act of 1601 made every parish in England and Wales responsible for the relief of its own poor.[1] In doing so it followed the tradition of earlier poor law legislation which had treated poor relief as a charitable act to be administered through ecclesiastical machinery whose local unit was the parish.[2] The parish was also well suited to the task which it had to perform, for over much of England the parish was coterminous with a single village community. This meant that each social and economic unit was expected to undertake the relief of its own poor, a simple, practical arrangement which placed the responsibility on those who could be expected to recognise the moral claim upon them. The advantages of the parish as a unit are clearly demonstrated when one looks at those places where it proved unsatisfactory because it did not represent a single clearly defined community. There were two groups of such parishes with contrasting characteristics.

First there were the rural areas of the North and West of England and Wales where the pattern of settlement and ecclesiastical boundaries did not form the neat pattern to be found in the Midlands and the South. Even where the nucleated village settlement pattern was present, several such units were gathered into one extensive parish and there were many areas where villages did not exist, the parish being simply an agglomeration of tiny hamlets. In such circumstances the unit of administra-

34

tion did not coincide with a single social and economic community, but included several, and so opened the way to jealousy and argument. People were less willing to contribute to the maintenance of distant paupers whom they did not know than to those in their own community, but were always ready to press the claims of their own poor neighbours to a share of the funds they were obliged to raise.[3] The size of these parishes also made administration more difficult; the overseers' task was much harder if both ratepayers and paupers were scattered over a wide area so that they could not know them personally. It was sixty years before parliament remedied this anomaly by the simple expedient of enacting that, where the parishes were extensive, each township should be responsible for its own poor.[4] The term township was less precisely defined than parish but implied a single settlement. Thus the large parish areas were given the same system of administration as the rest of the county. The disadvantage of this was that it could be carried to extremes. Where hamlet settlement was the norm a township might contain no more than two or three households but have power to rate itself and relieve its own poor. This was the *reductio ad absurdum*. Tiny units like this could only use the simplest methods of distributing relief and the multiplicity of units which this fragmentation implied served to complicate the problems of deciding where paupers were settled.

At the other extreme the parish proved equally unsuitable as a unit of administration where it was smaller than, and a subdivision of, the social and economic community. This was true in most towns and appeared at its worst in the larger and older ones where parishes tended to be both numerous and small. In contrast with the position in country areas the nomination of the parish as the unit of administration here represented a break with the past. In the sixteenth century the towns had led the way in establishing public relief systems but this had been done by the corporations as part of their responsibility for the welfare of the town as a whole.[5] At best, parochial officers had been subordinate local officers. This arrangement, like parochial responsibility in rural areas, placed the burden on a single eco-

nomic and social unit but the legislation of 1601 brought it to
an end. True, the corporations retained an interest in poor relief
through their duties as charity trustees and through the magisterial responsibilities to suppress vagrancy and supervise the
parochial officers. It is also clear that tradition, bolstered by these
specific powers, enabled many corporations to play an important
part in organising poor relief during the seventeenth century.[6]
But they had no legal powers for control or direction, and the
parish overseers became increasingly independent in the exercise
of their statutory powers. This fragmentation was unsatisfactory
in several respects; in a town people moved about from parish
to parish more often than in the country which meant that a
good deal of effort had to be devoted to keeping track of settlements.[7] Different social classes tended to congregate in different
areas so that one parish might have a strong financial base and
few poor while another had numerous poor and few substantial
ratepayers; many parishes were small and without the resources
needed to offer the more sophisticated forms of relief such as
workhouses. In short, the seventeenth century saw the urban
relief authorities become both fragmented and weak.

The problem became so serious in some towns that attention
was directed to seeking a solution which would enable these
various bodies to work together in harmony. That which emerged
involved a radical departure from earlier practice and marked a
major advance in the administrative methods of relief authorities.
This was the local act of parliament by which a particular place
could free itself from the administrative system laid down for it
by the law of the land, and establish one more appropriate to
its own local needs. The first town to obtain such an act was
Bristol. This act and those for other towns which followed it
are best known for their workhouse provisions but they are no
less important for the way in which they brought together the
municipal corporations and representatives of each parish in a
single authority responsible for all aspects of poor relief within
the town. Since these authorities had substantial financial resources and were responsible for large numbers of poor they were
both willing and able to execute ambitious schemes for housing,

feeding and employing the poor. Throughout the remainder of our period the grouping of parishes into more viable units remained one of the objects sought by the urban and rural parishes which applied for local acts.[8]

The parish then was least appropriate as a unit of administration in the upland hamlets of the North and West and the populous urban centres, but even in the greater part of the country, where the parish or township comprised a single village community, combination or union was found to be useful for certain purposes. The most outstanding of these was the establishment of workhouses. We shall be looking at the way in which these institutions were managed and the advantages which unions brought in Chapter 5.[9] Here it is only necessary to consider briefly the constitutional arrangements between the participating parishes.

With the exception of a few early examples these workhouse unions were formed under the provisions of either the 1722 Workhouse Act[10] or Gilbert's Act of 1782.[11] The latter laid down a precise administrative structure. It specified what officers there should be, their duties and their mode of appointment. The financial arrangements were similarly indicated and parishes forming unions under this act naturally conformed more or less to its provisions. The 1722 Act allowed the parishes to form their unions in whatever way they chose. Basically they took one of two forms. They either consisted of two or more parishes coming together as equals to unite for workhouse purposes or of one parish opening the doors of its workhouse to the poor of other parishes.[12] Once a union had been established it made little difference to the members which arrangement was in use. A parish wishing to join or leave a workhouse was little affected by whether it had to make terms and settle accounts with another parish or a corporate entity. The only difference was that the corporate system gave each parish a say in the running of the workhouse and at the same time imposed an obligation to see that it was well run. Many of the documents recording the agreements between parishes to set up these unions have come down to us.[13] Some, between groups of parishes constituting corporate

unions were formal indentures, others, perhaps only involving a
pair of adjacent parishes, might be noted on a leaf in a minute
book or on an odd scrap of paper. Whatever the form of agreement, the terms were concerned above all with two matters, the
constitutional arrangements and the financial arrangements. The
former involved the establishment of procedures which would
enable the ratepayers to exercise control over the organisation of
their institution and allow each constituent parish its due say in
corporate affairs. This usually required the formation of some
form of joint committee. The function and duties of such bodies
varied considerably, but in many places the unwillingness of lay
officers to become involved in the mundane details of administration meant that they were minimal.

The financial arrangements were more complex. There were
four factors to consider: overheads, maintenance costs, extras and
employment. The first included expenses incurred in the acqui-
sition and maintenance of the building, the payment of the
governor and other staff, and any other costs which had to be
met whether there were any poor in the house or not. These were
generally shared equally by all the participating parishes. The
maintenance costs were those essential to the support of the
pauper inmates: food, fire, washing, cleaning, etc. The total
weekly or monthly expenditure on these items was generally
divided among the number of inmates and each parish charged
for its own. The extras were any items pertaining to an individual
pauper over and above essential maintenance costs. They might
include the supply and repair of clothing, medical attention,
maternity services and funeral expenses. These were paid by
parishes as and when they were incurred by their own paupers.
Work involved a two-way transfer of funds—payments by the
parishes for materials and equipment and payment to them for
the earnings of their own poor.

The formation of workhouse unions was, as far as the administration of the old poor law went, in the development of
voluntary, as opposed to statutory, supra-parochial bodies. This
was an advance which enabled many rural parishes to use a
much wider range of relief methods than would otherwise have

been available to them, but it had severe limitations. Unions were very fragile because parishes could leave one union and join another whenever they chose. As a result it was difficult to maintain continuity of policy. The parishes using a particular workhouse need not be contiguous and were often spread over a wide area and had nothing in common but the workhouse itself. In many cases they did not even share the same objectives. Workhouses could be used in so many ways that neighbouring parishes might have quite contradictory views as to the purpose and functions of their common institutions.[14]

The difficulties which had to be overcome by those seeking to build viable supra-parochial institutions were not the greatest price which had to be paid for the convenience of the parish as the unit of adminstration. This was imposed by the burden of settlement administration which the system of localised relief demanded. We have already seen how, in the second half of the seventeenth century, parliament evolved a legal framework which allowed parishes to remove to their place of settlement those who were actually or potentially chargeable while allowing people to gain settlement in the parish of their adoption by fulfilling certain conditions, or to remain undisturbed until chargeable if they brought a certificate from their place of settlement. Here we are concerned with the way the parishes put these regulations into effect.

First, it must be remembered that parishes were familiar with the problem of settlement long before 1662. The legislation of that and subsequent years was introduced to strengthen their hand and regularise the procedures for actions which had formerly been taken under inadequate and inappropriate laws. Usually parishes had relied upon the 1589 *Act Against Erecting and Maintaining Cottages*.[15] The purpose of this statute was to reduce rural poverty by preventing the over-population of villages where opportunities for employment were restricted by the availability of land. Thus it enacted that no cottages might be built unless four acres of land were put with them and the keeping of lodgers was prohibited. Exceptions were made for corporate and market towns, maritime districts and places dependent upon extractive industries where an influx of labour might be desirable and the availability of land was irrelevant. The enforcement of this act was entrusted to manor courts and it is in their records in the sixteenth and well on into the seventeenth century that one finds regular references to amercements being levied for keeping inmates. In some cases they are so frequent as to be more a licence fee than a penalty. The boroughs and industrial areas excepted from the provisions of this act pursued a similar policy relying on local bylaws to expel newcomers or to demand from them bonds for the reimbursement of the parish should they become chargeable. The frequency with which they were obliged to act suggests that not only was movement widespread but that these attempts to stem the tide were far from successful. In fact very little research has been done on this early history of removal. There is much more we should like to know about local differences in approach, whether particular types of parish were most concerned about it or if some districts showed little interest.[16]

In 1662 the administration of settlement was placed on the same footing everywhere and the surviving archives of numerous parishes are ample evidence of the activity and paper work it demanded. The bond for the security of the parish was authorised by the 1662 Act but its heyday was earlier and it is most frequently found in town records from the first half of the century.[17] It was only worth taking bonds from better-off people and the new legislation made provision for them to gain new settlements. The certificate, made widely available by the 1697 Act, was a similar but more effective alternative to the bond. Very few of the temporary certificates available earlier have survived but numerous parishes in all parts of the country accumulated files of certificates between 1697 and the reforms of 1795. They also accumulated similarly bulky files of removal orders and less frequently of the examinations to which paupers were subjected in order to determine their place of settlement. After 1795 the quantity of paper connected with removal increased. There were orders of suspension made when the pauper was too sick to travel, as was often the case, correspondence, and papers dealing with the financial arrangements between the parishes involved.[18]

All these records are evidence of the system at work, evidence that people were moving about, and that they were liable to removal in their time of need. But they deserve a more thorough investigation than they have so far received. It would be illuminating to look at the certificates and removal orders in conjunction with parish registers and other local records to discover the subsequent history of certificate men and the earlier history of removees. Did the former stay long? Were they eventually removed, or did their children gain new settlements as apprentices or servants and render the certificate a dead letter? Were those removed before they became chargeable newcomers for whom a certificate was unobtainable or unacceptable? Were there any regular points of difference between those thus removed and those whose certificates were accepted? Provoked by the examinations, with their real-life case-histories, a stream of questions comes to mind which demonstrates the significance of settlement papers to a far wider field of social history than poor relief alone.[19]

Although the settlement system worked with tolerable efficiency within the channels laid down by law there were cases of extreme action for both good and ill. The former are found less frequently and the most notable example was the anticipation of the 1795 reforms by the earlier introduction of non-resident relief, substituting the transmission of paper and money for the transportation of people.[20] It was evidently beneficial to the pauper to be allowed to remain in familiar surroundings during sickness and old age but the system relied very heavily on good-will and trust between overseers and it is not surprising that most of the evidence for it comes from the industrial districts where there was relatively less clamour for economy on every account. In parishes where the finances were strained we often find a far less flexible approach to settlement which in a few cases degenerated into an obsessional perversity. Some parishes flatly refused to give any hostages to the future in the form of certificates. Others kept careful records of all certificates and removal orders given or received, or were prepared to spend the equivalent of several years' maintenance in litigation to prove that a pauper's settlement lay elsewhere. Litigation over settlement matters was inevitable. The sums of money at stake were not, over a period of years, trivial and the legislature, in laying down the framework, could not anticipate the strange circumstances in which people found themselves which might become relevant to settlement dispute, perhaps decades later. Appeals to quarter sessions were frequent and while some cases of unusual difficulty might lead to excessive and costly litigation, others produced compromise agreements.

The settlement laws were an inevitable consequence of a localised system of poor relief. They consumed time, energy and resources which would have been better devoted to relief itself but since it is doubtful whether the alternative of a nationally financed, bureaucratically administered system would have even been possible, let alone cheaper, this was simply part of the price which had to be paid for an effective relief system.

As a unit of administration the parish was, at best, a compromise. It was alike inappropriate in the most thinly populated rural areas and the densely populated towns, but for many villages and country towns where it did coincide with a single unit of settlement it could not be bettered. With the limited administrative resources available in the early sixteenth century it had to be local and pay the price of localisation in the form of settlement laws. But there were compensations. Administrative costs were reduced to a minimum and in most places the ratepayers and the paupers were known to each other. This was conducive both to effective control of expenditure and fair treatment of the poor. It was difficult to feign poverty amongst one's neighbours or to grind the faces of the poor if they lived next door. Parish officers were often able to break out of the parochial strait-jacket if it impeded the pursuit of desirable objectives. Certain types of parish and particular localities, though, let it be admitted, by no means all, made full use of the local act procedure and voluntary unions to equip themselves with supra-parochial machinery of institutions which enabled them to escape from some of the limitations imposed by the parochial system.

Administration and Finance

Within each parish or township the administration of poor relief
was entrusted to officers appointed for that purpose subject to the
general supervision of the ratepayers assembled in a vestry
meeting. Until the 1601 Act these officers were to be the churchwardens serving *ex officio* and two, three or four overseers of the
poor to be chosen annually.[21] Generally the churchwardens'
service was nominal and the duties fell entirely upon the shoul-
ders of the overseers, of which most parishes had two. They
were selected by the vestry or, as occurred in some parishes
during the seventeenth century, the manor court,[22] and the formal appointment was made by the magistrates. Although many
vestries went through the motions of an annual election it is
clear that most villages had a rota or house-row system under
which the occupiers of the main properties in the parish served in
a predetermined order.[23] If a woman was occupying a property
on the rota she was expected to serve although the legality of
this was questioned from time to time.[24] In towns the elections
had more substance. With many more properties and ratepayers
to consider, it was less easy to maintain a traditional rota and
the vestries were often obliged to find someone to serve each
year.

In most parishes, both town and country, the overseers worked
together as a team but in a few it was the custom to divide the
duties between them. Thus they might each take part of the
parish or part of the year or one collect the money and the other
pay it out.[25] Overseers of the poor have come in for a good deal
of criticism both from their contemporaries and from subsequent
historians. Indeed, it is easy to draw up a list of their faults and
failings and it was especially so for Richard Burn, one of the
best known of these writers, who as a magistrate, came most into
contact with the overseers when things had gone wrong, when
disputes arose and when litigation was being pursued.[26] That such
failings existed cannot be denied. What is less certain is how

widespread they were. It is true that each year new overseers
came into office with no immediate executive experience, but
most of them would have served before and be familiar with the
present position from attendance at vestry meetings. They were
not being swept into an office of which they had no knowledge
but serving their turn, as an active member of the continuing,
and often close-knit body, which ruled the parish. Their main
duty was to keep running a system which had a momentum of
its own and in which most problems could be solved by reference
to past experience and precedent. Of course there were overseers
who neglected their duties and left a mess at the end of the year
for their successors to clear up. Critics have tended to overlook
the fact that a good deal depended upon the personality of the
overseer. Some were conscientious and able, others idle and in-
incompetent. We hear more of the latter because their failings
had undesirable consequences but it does not follow that they
were the more numerous. One might say that the failures of the
poor law administration lay not in the wholesale negligence of
its officers but in a tendency to lose momentum imperceptibly
over a period of years which also saw a growth in the size of the
problem and thus culminated in a crisis which forced the vestry
to inaugurate reforms or a change of policy. Continuing steady
activity punctuated by bouts of reform and improvement is the
pattern which we find in parish after parish.[27]

In some parts of the country, overseers who did not wish to
perform the routine duties in person appointed and paid a
deputy to serve on their behalf. Very little is known about the
incidence of this practice and, indeed, we are only aware of it
in those places where the deputy had sufficient status to be mentioned as such in the records. If he did everything in the name
of his employer we should be quite ignorant of the matter. The
hiring of personal deputies was one of the roots from which grew
the idea of the parish employing staff to perform the routine
duties on behalf of the annual overseers. When most of the overseers were employing deputies and many of them choosing the
same man it was natural to put this chance improvement in
administrative continuity on a formal basis by employing a per-

manent parish officer.[28] The other root from which parish staffs grew was the workhouse governor. In many places he was the first and only paid officer and it often seemed reasonable to give him duties not connected with the workhouse such as collecting rates, keeping accounts and paying pensions. In populous parishes the staff tended to grow to keep pace with the duties and there was increasing specialisation among the salaried officers. There is much that we still need to learn about the emergence and development of parish staffs. As in so many other developments the towns, where the pressure of work was greatest, led the way, but there is some evidence to suggest considerable regional variations in the extent to which smaller parishes made use of paid officers. If research is to throw light on these problems it must consider an area large enough to allow the identification of regional trends, customs and policies.

All these developments took place without any sanction in law. It was not until 1819 that legislation sponsored by Sturges Bourne specifically gave parishes the power to hire paid officers who were to be called assistant overseers.[29] The interest in paid officers manifested in this act was sustained into the 1820s, when requests for information from parishes regularly included a question as to the existence of an assistant overseer. The results were published along with other information in a series of county totals.[30] These give some indication of the popularity of paid officers in different parts of the country and the trend of the figures may show whether they proved successful and an encouragement to other parishes to make appointments or whether they proved to be a costly failure dropped after a trial period. One thing these figures do not tell us is the precise effect of Sturges Bourne's Act. We have no figures for the number of parishes with paid officers before its enactment and many of these would be included in the returns because their officers were regarded as or even called assistant overseers or because the parish adopted the new statutory procedures for appointment in respect of a long-standing office. Nor do the returns give any indication of the size of parish staffs. A parish with a part-time assistant overseer might have more in common with one having no staff than with a large town employing a vestry clerk, rate collectors, book-keepers, cashiers and so on, but for the purpose of the returns they both counted as assistant overseer parishes.

What exactly were the duties of these officers? Quite simply they were the collection of money from ratepayers, its distribution among the poor and the keeping of accounts of receipts and disbursements. Other tasks built up around these. If ratepayers witheld money, overseers had to approach the magistrates and deal with the formalities needed to compel payment. When people sought relief, the overseer had to decide whether they were entitled to it and to attend the magistrates if the applicant appealed against a negative decision. If newcomers entered the village the overseers had to collect their settlement certificates or arrange for their removal and be prepared to organise the litigation which an appeal might produce. When illegitimate children were born the overseers had to obtain bonds from, or affiliation orders against, the putative father and collect the money due. Listed like this the duties of overseers seem both onerous and varied but some tasks arose infrequently and many overseers got through their year of office without meeting the more obscure and difficult aspects of the job.[31]

The records created and accumulated by the overseers in the course of their work were so closely bound up with various aspects of poor relief that they will be fully discussed in that context.[32] Suffice only to say here that these are the records of poor relief *par excellence* and that pride of place among them must be given to the overseers' accounts. Since poor relief was essentially a matter of expenditure the accounts detail everything of importance which a parish did for its poor. As a result they are daunting both in their bulk and in the appearance of dull repetitiveness which their contents present. In fact they are the source which, more than any other, will lead, when we understand how to exploit them, to a fuller and deeper understanding of how poor relief was carried out at the parochial level.

The overseers were appointed and supervised by vestry meetings which all ratepayers could attend. As a rule this supervision was limited to auditing the accounts at the end of the year but in towns and other parishes where the growth of population made the intimate everybody-knowing-everybody-else atmosphere a thing of the past, it was often found necessary for the vestry to meet more regularly, or for the annual vestry to appoint a committee to help the overseer in his work. The main task of such bodies was adjudicating applications for relief. The overseer was relegated from taking decisions to making inquiries and giving the vestry reports on each claimant's circumstances as a basis on which the decision might be taken. The minutes of vestry meetings are very valuable when they record the evolution of policy, but in dealing with claims for relief they generally give names and decisions yet omit details of the financial circumstances which would convert a dull routine record into an invaluable source of information. As with assistant overseers it was not until the second decade of the nineteenth century that the legislature took an interest in these supervisory committees. Sturges Bourne's Act of 1819[33] established a formal procedure whereby parishes might elect what amounted to standing committees to carry out the same sort of supervisory work which the various ad hoc committees of earlier years had performed. Undoubtedly legislation stimulated the spread of select vestries. This was especially so in the more thinly populated rural parishes where there had formerly been little interest, although careful supervision and control was clearly essential to any attempt to stamp out the problems associated with the Speenhamland System. The spread of select vestries in the 1820s is noted in the returns that record the assistant overseers and is subject to the same provisos.[34]

Of the various tasks which the parish vestries and officers had to undertake, one of the simplest was raising the necessary money, though even that was not without its complications. The 1601 Act said that this should be done by taxing all occupiers of property within the parish according to their ability to pay. There is some evidence that at first parishes did try to rate their inhabitants on the basis of ability to pay but it was an imprecise principle which could lead to endless argument and the tendency was to settle for some standard basis of assessment. All sorts of systems were tried at first.[35] In Lancashire it was the traditional

assessment for the parliamentary fifteenth;[36] in the Midlands the
tax was based on the number of yardlands in the open fields
each inhabitant occupied.[37] These systems brought some sort of
order into the rating system but they were static and were not
easily adapted to changing property values. As a result more and
more parishes chose to use the rental value of property as a basis
of assessment. This allowed new properties and improvements
to be reflected in the valuation year by year. On the whole this
system worked reasonably well. Property was a fairly good indication of wealth and any attempt to assess ability to pay more
precisely would have required much more work and would have
generated more disputes.

There were certain places where the rental system did prove
unsatisfactory. One was the ports and other centres of mercantile activity. Here a good deal of wealth was tied up, not in real
property, but in stock-in-trade and in ships moored at the quay-
sides. This was a constant source of trouble. On the whole the
weight of legal opinion was that these types of property were
rateable but in practice they were difficult to assess, there being
no equivalent of the rental value. As a result officers tended to
neglect or under-rate them and to break with long-standing local
custom by seeking to charge their full value only when especially
hard-pressed. We see the results in the series of disputes and
lawsuits that punctuate the poor law history of several mercantile
parishes.[38]

The Industrial Revolution brought another group of problems.
Mills and factories could be easily rated on the rental system,[39]
but what about canals and railways that only generated profits
over a length extending through several parishes by means of tolls
payable at their termini? Some were exempt from rates by the
statutes which established them, but there was considerable
argument as to whether others should pay rates to each parish
through which they passed for the enhanced value of their land
or whether they were only rateable in those parishes where tolls
were actually collected.[40] The most serious anomaly of the rating
system concerned the extractive industries. It was held that,
because the Act of 1601 specifically mentioned coal mines, all

other mines were excluded on account of their highly speculative
nature and loss-making tendencies. This exemption did not
extend to quarrying for stone, lime and slate or to salt pits or
mineral spa water or to those enjoying duties on mineral production without taking any of the mining risks, but the exemption
of the mines themselves was a cause of much resentment. It was
at its greatest in connection with the extraction of non-ferrous
metals. These mines tended to be in mountainous, backward and
thinly populated parts of the countryside where agriculture was
primitive and its profits were small. When mines were opened up
they attracted people who might in due course gain settlements.
Mining activity fluctuated greatly and the parish had to support
those who were laid off if the mine flooded or the proprietors
could not sell their produce or went bankrupt and had to close
the mine. Since it was the occupiers of property, the farmers and
the shopkeepers who had to pay the rates this was a clear case of
one sector causing poverty for which another had to pay.[41] A
further anomaly brought about by industrialisation concerned
housing for the new urban workers. These people had low incomes which by tradition would entitle them to exemption from
paying poor rates. This meant the property was yielding substantial profits to its owners while contributing nothing to the common burdens.

Attempts to remedy these defects in the rating system were
mostly left to local initiative. Parishes regularly included provisions governing rating in their local acts. These could deal
with stock-in-trade, small tenements and other matters so that
the financial arrangements in a local act parish might be markedly
different from those in the country as a whole. One of the few
anomalies which was remedied at national level was the small
tenement problem. An act passed in 1818 enabled parishes to
charge some landlords by fixing a composition rate for the whole
property.[42]

By making each parish responsible for its own finance, parliament revealed another weakness of the parochial system. There
was no certainty that there would be an even balance between
the supply of money and the demand for relief. In practice,

D

problems only arose in extreme cases. The average village or town was a balanced community which could find money to relieve the numbers of poor likely to arise within it. We have already seen that towns might have a wealthy parish where the affluent congregated and much poorer ones with a mainly labouring population.[43] Other places might be subject to enormous pressure on the rates at a particular time if a local enterprise had closed, creating severe local unemployment. The Act of 1601 did make provision for situations of this kind by giving magistrates power to levy a rate on one parish in aid of another. This power was used quite widely in the early seventeenth century both to assist towns where plague had brought economic life to a standstill and to support those made destitute by industrial depressions. Naturally, it caused a good deal of resentment and seems to have fallen into disuse after the Restoration.[44]

In short, the rating system based eventually on the rental valuation had all the strengths and weaknesses of the parochial system as a whole. For most of the country, where the township or parish coincided with a single economic and social community it was adequate for its purpose. Like the whole structure of unpaid officers supervised by local vestries it was simple, convenient and effective. In multi-parish towns, on the other hand, it merely served to emphasise the disadvantages of taking responsibility for poor relief from the town government and giving it to the parish. Similarly it was the vast, unforeseeable changes wrought by the Industrial Revolution that revealed the weaknesses of the traditional rating system as part of the process by which they laid bare the inadequacies of a system created to meet the simpler needs of an earlier age.

Notes to this chapter are on pages 126–9

Chapter 3
Poverty and the Poor

So far we have been concerned with the legal and administrative arrangements for poor relief. Now we must examine the way in which the parochial authorities set about performing the tasks assigned to them. In doing so the first question to be asked is who was eligible for poor relief? It is a question in which modern historians have as much interest as did the overseers and vestry-men who first asked it. For much of the time the latter could work by custom, precedent and unwritten rule of thumb, but if we are to understand their methods and their policies we must be able to see in terms of facts (ages, occupations, incomes, disabilities and so on) and figures (numbers and proportions) what they saw as individual people with personal problems. No quest is more vital to an appreciation of what the overseers were doing and none illustrates better the possibilities and limitations of the records which they created in the transaction of routine businesses.[1] The problem of eligibility therefore merits a detailed examination not only because of its intrinsic importance but because it illustrates so well how the research student must draw on a wide range of sources and the problems which he will meet in seeking to extract useful information from them.

The records of poor law administration have come down to us in great quantities but they tell us remarkably little about the poor themselves and the circumstances which brought them into dependence on poor relief. The reasons for this are not far

to seek. The legal and practical necessities which induced the
compilation and preservation of records relating to policy and
administration did not apply with the same force when it came
to the poor themselves. When records were made it was to give
actions legal validity or to prevent fraud. This applies to the
statutes which established and governed the development of the
poor law, to the formal documents recording the appointment of
officers, committees and staff, to the codes of rules which defined
their duties and governed their conduct, to the minutes and
accounts which record policy decisions, how relief was to be
allocated and the way in which the money was spent. It is only
in these last two that we come into contact with the poor themselves but even then the information is generally restricted to
names. Even if an applicant's circumstances had been thoroughly
investigated before relief was given the decision alone was recorded. It was only in the populous parishes that such formal
inquiries were needed and it was there that the large number
of cases being dealt with demanded brevity in recording. For the
most part, however, poor law authorities were small rural parishes
where everyone knew everyone else. Overseers and vestries
reached their decisions on the basis of common knowledge and
the mention of a name in the accounts was sufficient to justify
the expenditure to auditing ratepayers.

Since the normal routine records of poor relief administration
are generally silent on this crucial question it becomes necessary
to turn to less usual sources in search of detailed information.
This is unfortunate because by their very nature they tend to
deal with atypical situations. On the other hand they offer a
wealth of information not available elsewhere which cannot be
ignored.

One occasion on which the detailed information which we are
seeking was recorded was at the establishment of a new administration, when those undertaking responsibility for poor
relief sought to assess the magnitude of their problem. Such was
the case in the late sixteenth and early seventeenth century when
public relief was first becoming established. This period saw the
production of two of the best lists of paupers yet to appear in

print, those of Ipswich[2] and Norwich.[3] Both towns were heavily
dependent on the textile industry and were among the first to be
forced to take positive action to deal with poverty. A more general
account of poverty in the early seventeenth century can be con-
structed from the petitions addressed to the court of quarter
sessions by paupers seeking relief. In them the applicants described their condition and although allowance has to be made
for a tendency to exaggerate factors favourable to their case they
give a useful indication of the level of poverty which was thought
to merit relief. As poor relief became firmly established more and
more people found that an application to the overseers was
enough and, as the seventeenth century drew to a close, the tendency was for petitions to come only from borderline cases and
those who were exceptionally persistent or perverse though, if
one could discriminate between these two, quarter sessions petitions would remain a useful indication of the borderline of
pauperism.[4] These early lists and petitions can be used in conjunction with similar information recorded by some boards of
guardians when they took over responsibility for the administration of poor relief in the years after 1834.[5] Thus we not only have
information about the level of poverty thought to confer eligibility for relief in two important periods but the means of making
a comparison between the two.

For the intervening period we must rely on accounts of the
poor compiled in connection with reforms of the administration
or attempts to reduce the numbers in receipt of relief. Local
initiatives of this sort can be found from all periods, but occasionally there were more widespread movements for reform.
One example dates from the 1690s—a decade which saw a run
of bad harvests, widespread distress, soaring relief expenditure
and a series of enactments designed to reduce the number of
paupers and the cost of relief. All parish vestries were instructed
to revise their pension lists annually. This ensured that people
whose circumstances had improved were taken off the list and
that parish money was not wasted on the undeserving or at the
mere whim of an overseer. Parishes did not normally state in their
records that they were revising the pension list in accordance

with this statute,[6] but it is often clear that they were doing so well
into the eighteenth century. As a result the pension list became
in many places a regular and distinct branch of relief expenditure.[7] This is most apparent in overseers' accounts where the
first item is the pension list and it is followed by the miscellaneous expenditure. The distinction is even clearer when there
are separate headings: 'pensioners', 'casual poor', 'expenses', etc.
Another method of curbing the pension list which was made
compulsory during the 1690s was the wearing by the poor of a
badge bearing the letter P and the initial of their parish. Penalties
were laid on officers who failed to supply badges and paupers
who refused to wear them. It was hoped that by making the
identity of the paupers well known it would be more difficult
for them to make false claims undetected. It is difficult to assess
the immediate impact of this legislation because so few records
have survived. On the whole it seems that the act was obeyed at
first but that badges slowly fell into disuse to be revived from
time to time throughout the eighteenth century when parishes
were seeking to reform their administration and tighten their
control of the poor. There were several reasons for the minimal
use made of the badge system. In small parishes where common
knowledge was already doing the job for which badges were intended it was hard to justify the expense and effort involved in
obtaining badges and ensuring that they were worn. The problem of enforcement was even greater in the towns where those
at whom the badge scheme was directed could probably evade
its provisions without too much difficulty. Thus badges could
easily become an indignity to the deserving without being a
menace to imposters. Badges had all but disappeared by the
time the relevant legislation was repealed in 1810.[8]

This disappearance of badges mattered little because a new and
more effective means of achieving the same end had now been
discovered. This was the printed list of paupers distributed by
the parish among the ratepayers, an idea which emerged in the
towns where it was impossible for the overseers to keep track of
all their numerous poor. They had to enlist the aid of all ratepayers in identifying the minority who would feign sickness or

unemployment, collect their relief and then go off to remunerative employment, perhaps in another parish. Then as now, those
concerned to promote economy entertained exaggerated hopes of
the savings which weeding out malingerers might achieve and the
popularity of the printed list is a good indication of how widespread these hopes were. They have not survived in as great
numbers as one might expect. Overseers rarely thought to file a
copy with the parish records and most of the documents which
have come down to us have turned up in unexpected places. It
is often clear that they formed part of a series, and references in
minutes and accounts to lists that have not survived confirm our
suspicion that the available documents represent the tip of an
iceberg.[9]

Perhaps a word of warning is necessary here. When considering
both printed lists of paupers and badging, it is important to
avoid confusing the motives behind these schemes with the ideas
which governed poor relief policy after 1834. In the latter period
policies were framed with the deliberate intention of imparting
a stigma to pauperism but the badges and the lists were aimed
quite specifically at a deceitful minority. The words of the 1697
statute declaring its intention 'that the money raised only for the
relief of such as are well impotent as poor, may not be mis-
applied and consumed by the idle, sturdy and disorderly beggars'[10] were echoed in the words with which the overseer of
Castle Sowerby, Cumberland concluded his list of paupers in
1836: 'In laying the foregoing list before the public the Overseer
has to request that where the relief given to any of the above
Paupers appears to be objectionable, suggestions should at once
be made to him, and he begs to state that he will receive them
thankfully.'[11]

Towards the end of our period, as interest in the old poor law
and its problems grew, a number of investigators gathered and
published information about the nature of poverty. Eden was a
pioneer of this type of inquiry and his findings remain the most
comprehensive and widely available survey. He gathered his information during his travels in the years 1794–6 but as he could
only reproduce what others chose to tell him there is no stan-

dardisation in the presentation of his data. Thus we find various combinations of names, ages, descriptions and relief given, some of which are more useful than others.[12] Forty years later similar information was gathered by the Royal Commission, both through its parochial returns and its assistant commissioners. For the purposes of this analysis the returns are of limited value because they tend to be brief and set out in whatever way the respondent chose. They give very little information and less that is amenable to comparison. Only a minority of the assistant commissioners chose to gather and reproduce lists of poor in particular parishes and we must bear in mind the probability that they chose examples which illustrated and supported their general argument. The returns and lists are valuable evidence about the places to which they refer but whether one can generalise from them is another matter.[13]

The establishment or reform of an administration, the curtailing of expenditure and fraud, and research and investigation are the main situations in which detailed lists of paupers, together with accounts of their circumstances, were compiled. They all tend to suffer from the same defect of over-recording the urban areas at the expense of the more typical rural ones. It was the populous parishes which most needed written information as a basis for administrative changes and financial control and men like Eden tended to visit the main centres rather than villages off the beaten track. The question which arises, therefore, is how the investigation of rural poverty can discover something of the circumstances of the people whose names appear year in and year out in the accounts and minutes which are the staple of poor law records. This can only be done in the wider context of a detailed study of the social and economic structure of a particular parish, drawing on the full range of local sources and employing family reconstruction and other modern techniques.[14] Overseers' accounts have an important part to play in such an analysis. They tell us who was being relieved and for how long. It should be possible to estimate what proportion of the population the poor formed and to ascertain whether certain families remained on the fringes of pauperism for lengthy periods, regularly needing assistance in the poverty-prone phases of childhood, child rearing and old age. There is a good deal of work to be done on rural poverty, though it will be a slow process.

The Analysis of Poverty

With a variety of sources and techniques at his disposal an investigator can reasonably expect to obtain some information about the nature of poverty in the locality or period which interests him. Having found his sources, his next problem is to analyse their contents in a way which is both meaningful and permits comparison between one set of data and another. Naturally those who compiled our sources did not have such considerations in mind and they only recorded what they needed. Sometimes we only have the names, ages and relief of heads of households. Other compilers added addresses, non-relief income, notes on disabilities, reasons for needing relief and similar information for dependents. To make this amorphous mass of information meaningful it is essential to devise some scheme of classification. We can start with the distinction made in the 1601 Act between those able to work and those who could not. As we shall see when we come to look at the way overseers dealt with the able-bodied poor, it is possible to subdivide this category in several ways, but for present purposes it can be treated as a single group.

There were three main conditions which rendered people unable to work. The first was sickness which, used in its broadest sense, includes all forms of mental and physical disability both temporary and permanent. We can only be aware of these conditions if the sources specifically inform us. In many cases they do, because such conditions were also less readily apparent to those reading the lists. The second condition causing inability to work was old age. Here the problem is one of definition. Different people age at different speeds and the old poor law had no fixed retirement age. People became eligible for relief when advancing years rendered them unable to support themselves and their dependents unaided. But if we are to make any progress we must select some number of years beyond which it is reasonable to expect that age at least contributed to the cause of dependence. None will be perfect, fix the threshold too high and many aged poor will be excluded, place it too low and a greater number of non-aged cases will be included. Since the old poor law was a flexible system treating each case on its merits we cannot avoid a certain amount of overlap in any scheme of classification. On the whole the balance of advantage seems to be with the lowish age of fifty, which many of the respondents to the 1832 questionnaire seem to have used as the threshold of old age. When due allowance has been made for the strenuous life, limited diet and poor medical services of the period it would seem about the right age. The third group of poor who could not work for their support were the one-parent families headed by widows, deserted wives, unmarried mothers and, less frequently, widowers. Here the problem was not so much that the people involved were not able bodied as that one pair of hands could not do what normally required two. It was impossible to care for young children and work for their maintenance, and as a result one-parent families appear prominently and expensively in overseers' accounts.

Finally there was one group which fell on the borderline between able bodied and impotent poor; this consisted of children, most of whom came within the ambit of the poor law as a result of parental poverty, but there was a minority of orphans and children totally neglected by their parents, who became paupers in their own right. The overseers were responsible for their nurture as infants and for their education and employment when older. For purposes of analysis the age of fourteen has been taken as the upper limit of this group. It was the normal age for apprenticeship, though children were often bound out younger, even at half that age, and in parishes where domestic service was the only employment open to girls they were often several years older before a situation could be found for them.

These then were the main classes of deserving poor: the sick, the aged, one-parent families and children. We have met difficulties in arriving at a system of classification and it will not satisfy all, but it is far easier to achieve this than to attempt to classify the able-bodied poor. There was a world of difference between the problems of one man thrown out of work because of a falling demand for his particular skills and with little prospect of finding new work and several thousand laid off when a slump closed the mill that employed them, but sure of a job if they could survive until better conditions returned. Both examples can be classified as unemployment yet the main point of similarity is the difficulty overseers had in dealing with them. Furthermore, there were many conditions short of total unemployment which could impoverish a working man—underemployment, low wages, short-time working, an exceptionally large family to support. The circumstances of able-bodied poverty could be infinitely variable but the duty of the parish officers remained the same; it was to tide the victims over this difficult phase and take positive steps to facilitate an early return to independence.

The methods of identifying and classifying different kinds of poverty have been looked at in some detail because very little work has yet been done in this field in spite of the fact that a knowledge of the problem facing them is vital to any understanding of how the parochial authorities set about dealing with poverty. In the present state of knowledge it is impossible to describe the changing manifestations of poverty for the country as a whole. It is doubtful whether this would be desirable even if it were possible. The problem of poverty was a problem of matching local resources to local poverty and therefore what matters is the precise details of the local situation, not an aggregate of such local details purporting to reflect the national scene and effectively cancelling out the local variations which were its most significant feature. It may be useful to make several points, nevertheless. The first is the predominant position occupied by women in pension lists, especially in rural parishes before 1800. Whether they were aged, unsupported mothers or disabled, their prominence is striking and significant. Children were often the next most important group, followed by aged and infirm men and finally the able-bodied. The latter was in many ways a specialised form of poverty. It affected particular places

or particular people. Among the former were towns dependent
on industries vulnerable to cyclical fluctuations and districts
where a local manufacturing speciality was experiencing in-
exorable decline. Elsewhere able-bodied poverty often attached
to a particular individual who either had an exceptionally large
family to support or who had lost his employment and had
great difficulty finding another place. The second general point
is the way in which this picture changed in the last fifty years of
the old poor law. The onset of the Industrial Revolution greatly
expanded the area vulnerable to able-bodied poverty associated
with manufacture and caused the decline of many industries
which could not compete with the new mechanised factories. At
the same time, in many rural areas the problems associated with
the Speenhamland System are exemplified in the transformation
of pension lists at the turn of the century. Suddenly they are
much longer than in the eighteenth century and men's names
form the majority.

Within this outline we can find a picture of poverty infinitely
variable from place to place. Because poverty could adopt so
many different guises the means of dealing with it had to be no
less variable.

Notes to this chapter are on page 129

Chapter 4

Outdoor Relief

In the last chapter we considered how the 1601 Act divided the poor into two groups, the deserving and the able-bodied, and how for purposes of analysis these groups might be sub-divided into classes. In this and the next two chapters we shall be examining the various ways in which it was sought to relieve these different types of poverty. Firstly we shall be concerned with outdoor relief, the kind of relief envisaged in the 1601 Act, as it applied to the deserving poor. In the next chapter we shall look at the way in which institutions were developed as a means of obeying the injunction to employ the poor and how, in practice, these workhouses evolved into sanctuaries for the deserving poor which belied their name. Finally we shall look more closely at the problem of the able-bodied to examine the various methods of relief adopted and see how the problem eventually became so great as to destroy the old poor law.

First it will perhaps be useful to repeat a caveat made in the last chapter. When we consider poor relief we are forced to use categories to make the problem manageable, but this was not the way those actually involved were accustomed to think. They saw individuals who, for one reason or a combination of reasons, were unable to support themselves and their dependents. They did not see a category and determine their policy on that basis, they saw an individual with a problem to be solved in the most appropriate way.

Relief in Cash and in Kind

Throughout the period of the old poor law one method of giving relief stood out above all others as characteristic of the system. This was the pension, the regular, weekly, fortnightly or monthly cash payment. Although this becomes apparent after even the briefest examination of almost any of the vast mass of overseers' accounts which have survived, it has rarely received its due emphasis. In their all-embracing study the Webbs only deal with pensions in the relatively specialised context of a discussion of how overseers went about preventing the too rapid growth of the pension list and eliminating malingerers therefrom.[1] Others have treated pensions in an even more cursory manner.[2] There seem to be two reasons for this. In the first place, pensions paid to the elderly, widows, orphans and the chronic sick were and are uncontroversial. Contemporaries recognised such claims without demur and historians have not had sufficient information about the value of money and paupers' other resources to make an issue out of the level of the pensions paid.[3] Secondly, pensions did not create bulky records. Even in the accounts, it only needs as many lines as there were pensioners to record the name, weekly sum, number of weeks and annual total for each pensioner, while extras—casual relief, and administrative expenses—had to be set out individually and in detail. Very often the sums involved were trivial but they occupied by far the greater part of the account. The pensions were also pushed into the background by less important matters such as apprenticeship and illegitimacy which not only caused expenditure to be entered in the accounts but created special and bulky files of documents as well.

The pension acquired and retained its dominant position in the relief system because it had advantages for all concerned. To the overseers it was the simplest and most convenient way of distributing relief. To the recipient it offered the maximum choice in spending his income to meet needs which none knew better than he. The pension also had the advantage of flexibility. It could be quickly increased or reduced to meet changing circumstances such as growing families, improved employment opportunities in harvest time, and so on. As we shall see, it was also readily available to meet the needs of new types of poverty as they arose. Of course, these advantages were not necessarily exploited to the full. With a system relying on voluntary labour it would be surprising if they were, but the fact remains that the flexibility of the pension system contributed to the evolution of the relief system.

Although the pension remained the central bulwark against poverty it would be wrong to imply that even the permanent poor were never relieved in kind. The pamphleteers of the period kept up a running argument about the pros and cons of cash or kind. On the one hand it was argued that each pauper knew his own needs best and that a cash payment would enable him to meet them most efficiently. Against this it was asserted that money could be too easily dissipated in the beer house. Food and clothing were sure to go where they were needed. The crux of the argument turned on how one assessed the character of the paupers, but the outcome depended more on the character of the parish officer, who generally found that the pension was a simple and convenient method of distributing relief while the alternative involved much more work in selecting, buying, distributing goods and keeping the necessary books. Inertia combined with inconvenience to make the distribution of relief in kind a rare phenomenon. When it did occur it was usually as the last desperate throw of a parish willing to try anything that might stem the ever-rising tide of expenditure.[4] Usually when overseers became involved in the supply of food to the poor it was in times of crisis such as 1795 or 1800–1, when in many places food was made available free or at reduced prices to the wage-earning classes as a whole rather than to paupers alone.[5]

Of the basic necessities, housing was probably the one most frequently removed from the general cover of the pension and provided by the parish as a separate item. The usual reason for this was that rent was an annual or twice yearly payment.

Therefore there was always a danger that the pauper might fail
to save enough from his pension to pay it and be obliged to go
back to the parish for a supplementary payment to save him from
eviction. The simplest solution to this problem was for the
parish to undertake responsibility for rent and adjust the pension
accordingly.[6] Other parish officers found themselves providing
housing more directly because they happened to be landlords,
usually as trustees of some charitable bequest. Whether the
property had been given as part of an endowment or specifically
as a habitation for the poor it gave the parish a chance to escape
from unpredictable demands of private landlords. Other parishes
were so convinced of the advantages of making direct provision
for the housing of paupers that they bought or built houses
specifically for this purpose.[7] This policy was not popular but it
recurs throughout the period. It is interesting because it is one
stage on the line of thought which led to the workhouse. The
latter had an advantage in that parishes were empowered to compel paupers to enter it and could thereby escape all liability for
the payment of rent. In fact one does find examples of the same
building being used alternately as a mere habitation for the poor
and as an organised institution.[8]

Related to the provision of housing itself were payments for
repairs to property.[9] It was appropriate that they should be paid
in addition to the pension because they were an unpredictable,
irregular and infrequent expense. Under the same heading might
be placed clothing[10] and perhaps fuel.[11] These occasional needs
made up the bulk of relief in kind. In the late sixteenth and early
seventeenth centuries when poor relief was new they were unusual, but the need for such occasional and casual grants soon
became apparent, and a century later they not only became
firmly established parts of the relief system but the most rapidly
expanding sector.

Pension lists grew slowly while the population did the same,
but in a time of rising living standards casual relief was subject
to pressure for expansion from two directions. First, a growing
range of goods and services came within the limits of what was
regarded as essential even for a pauper; second, an increasing

number of people, normally independent, were forced to turn to
the parish for occasional requirements which, though formerly
regarded as luxuries or even unavailable, were now seen as necessities. As overseers gave way to these pressures their accounts
became longer with more and more entries for occasional payments, usually but not always, in kind both to pensioners and to
non-regular poor.

Medical Relief

The supreme example of this process by which rising standards
broadened the scope of poor relief was in the field of medical
services.[12] The 1601 Act made no mention of the treatment, as
opposed to the maintenance, of the sick. At the time this was
reasonable because doctors were scarce compared with the manufacturers of traditional herbal remedies and the purveyors of
omnipotent quack medicines, and their services were only available to the wealthy. As the seventeenth century advanced the
numbers of physicians, apothecaries and surgeons increased and
a growing number of towns took steps to make their services
available to the poor. Where the towns led, the rural parishes
followed, so that by 1700 it is usual to find occasional payments
to doctors in overseers' accounts.[13] There were good reasons why
medical treatment should have been extended to the poor as soon
as it became available. The parish was responsible for supporting the sick and their families and, even if it required additional
expenditure, the sooner they could be cured and restored to independence the better. Once it had been accepted that the parish
should provide medical relief, it was natural to give it to the
aged and chronic sick who would never be able to support themselves again, but whose suffering might be relieved thereby. It
was also natural to extend it to those whose savings might have
seen them through a short illness but did not amount to the
payment of doctors' bills. Not only was this done as an insurance
against persistent illness and ultimate dependence but also in
order to maintain a standard of provision which had become

E

accepted as the necessary minimum. Thus the scope of relief had expanded in two directions—the level of provision had risen and the range of people within its purview had been extended.

In the first place, medical relief was provided by parishes paying doctors' bills on behalf of paupers and others thought eligible for this kind of assistance. This was organised in different ways from place to place. One parish might pay a variety of doctors separately for each patient while another chose to appoint a parish doctor who would submit an annual bill for all his work.[14] However they were submitted, doctors' bills presented the parish with the task of achieving control over expenditure and value for money in a new and difficult field. Everyone knew the cost of food, clothing and housing and it was easy for the layman to assess what was required for any particular pauper. With medical attention it was a different matter. The layman did not know what was needed to treat a particular case or whether the charges for drugs and attention were reasonable. In parishes where there was more than one doctor it was possible to maintain some degree of control through comparison and competition. This policy was often carried to its logical conclusion in the fixed-price contract. Many of the agreements which parishes reached with their doctors have come down to us. They were all very much alike. In them the doctor agreed to provide all the medical attention and drugs required by the parish poor during a specified time in return for a predetermined payment. Certain items were often excluded, the favourites being smallpox, midwifery and broken bones. For the last two, a fixed price per case was sometimes agreed.[15]

Although the arguments in favour of letting medical relief on contract were far stronger than those for giving all relief in this way, they were not overwhelming. If a doctor offered, and a parish accepted, a tender that was too low they deprived the poor of the required treatment and so defeated the object of the operation. Parishes were not slow to appreciate this point and contracts never became universal. They have been recorded from as early as the first quarter of the eighteenth century[16] but many parishes did not go over to this system until they found their finances under extraordinary pressure and were forced to find ways of reducing expenditure.[17] Others never resorted to the medical contract, or reverted to bill paying after a period of contracting.[18] In the past there has perhaps been a tendency to overemphasise the incidence of contracting and its attendant evils because the relevant agreements stand out as notable items in the records while the regular routine payments of doctors' bills goes unnoticed among all the other items which appear in overseers' accounts. Indeed unless the title 'doctor' is used they can only be identified if supporting vouchers have survived or one happens to know the names of the local practitioners. The relative importance of contracting and bill payment, the preferences of different localities and periods, and the chronology of changes from one to the other, remain to be worked out in detail.

Although the employment of surgeons, apothecaries and physicians to treat the poor in their own homes remained the normal method of providing medical relief throughout our period, it was certainly not the only one. From time to time other persons were employed to do specific jobs. They ranged from bone-setters and the purveyors of quack remedies[19] to midwives who played an important part in the medical services both for pauper women, chiefly unmarried mothers, and those in independent families whose resources would not run to what by the end of the eighteenth century had come to be regarded as a necessity.[20] When the treatment could not be brought to the poor they were sent to it at parish expense. In the appropriate localities overseers sent their poor both to the medical waters of the various spas[21] and to the sea to obtain the benefits of bathing in salt water.[22] In 1662 the Yorkshire magistrates even ordered a voluntary collection to send a Wakefield woman to London to be touched for the evil![23] These journeys were in search of traditional remedies but, as the eighteenth century advanced, paupers were very often sent away to take advantage of the latest improvements in medical treatment for the poorer classes. These were to be found in the various institutions whose establishment and continuance was a notable achievement of the charitable efforts in this period.

The most important of these were the infirmaries which were
established in nearly all the major provincial towns during the
second half of the eighteenth century.[24] They relied for their
capital on gifts and bequests and for their continuing income on
annual subscriptions which entitled the subscribers to nominate
patients in proportion to the sum given. Many parishes took
advantage of this facility.[25] The case of Manchester Infirmary
where a full series of annual reports has survived, can be taken
as an example.[26] When it opened in 1752 the nearest infirmary
was at Liverpool, but as the years went by the area it served
grew less as similar institutions were opened at Chester (1755),
Leeds (1767), Lancaster (1781), Sheffield (1797) and Bolton
(1814). Even so, in the years down to 1837 when the new unions
were established, seventy-seven parishes in Lancashire subscribed
for at least one year. Only the most populous, Salford, Bury,
Bolton, Oldham and Manchester itself remained subscribers for
the whole of this period. Others subscribed for two, three or
more years, some for fairly lengthy periods, or even for two or
three such spells with substantial breaks in between. It would
appear that while the contribution which the infirmary could
make to pauper health was widely recognised, only the larger
parishes were in a position to take full advantage of it. For others
the subscription was useful, but not essential; one of the first
things to be cut out when economy measures were required.

At the same time as the infirmaries were being established to
bring in-patient treatment to the poor, the dispensaries were
being opened to provide them with free drugs. They were
financed in the same way but, since they were less costly, smaller
communities could support them and they became more
numerous. Many parishes in and near the towns and market
centres where dispensaries were established took advantage of
their services, but much research remains to be done on the dispensaries before the full extent to which they were utilised by
poor law authorities can be assessed.[27]

After the general medical institutions came the specialised
ones. The most important of these were the lunatic asylums.
The mentally sick had been a burden on the poor rates from the

earliest days and had always proved a singularly difficult group
of paupers. Many were helpless and required the constant attention and assistance of others, which made them expensive to
maintain. Others were prone to violence and therefore unacceptable in their own homes.[28] This generally meant that the
overseers had to find room for them among the other poor in the
workhouse.[29] Occasionally a parish sought to do rather more by
sending a lunatic to a private madhouse[30] or to the Bethlehem
Hospital in London.[31] In the early eighteenth century these were
the only institutions where pauper lunatics might receive treatment and some came considerable distances to obtain it. At the
root of the problem lay ignorance. The plight of lunatics was not
understood and as a result they aroused fear and hatred rather
than compassion and sympathy. In this light we can understand
why so many lunatics housed in workhouses were chained up or
incarcerated in cells. The only alternative offering itself to the
overseer of limited knowledge and financial resources was to
allow them to run wild, disturbing and distressing the other
inmates.[32]

It was not until the second half of the eighteenth century that
the first attempts were made to establish public institutions in the
provinces where lunatics might be cared for in accordance with
their peculiar requirements and, if possible, treated. Among
them were charitable ventures such as the Retreat at York[33] and
asylums like those at Manchester and Liverpool, associated with
infirmaries but financed in a different way.[34] Their capital was
still provided by bequests and donations but the running expenses were paid by the friends, relatives or, in the case of
paupers, the parish of the lunatic. The number of such institutions grew steadily but they remained comparatively few, and
each served a limited locality only. Parishes were not compelled
to take advantage of their services and their heavy charges tended
to mean that they only received the most difficult cases, which
parishes were glad to be rid of whatever the cost. But, as so often
happens, voluntary action was the precursor of state intervention.
The voluntary lunatic asylums had shown that something could
be done for lunatics, that much more needed to be done and that

for many nothing would be done until the relief authorities
could be compelled to send their lunatics to asylums and meet
the cost. This was done by the County Asylum Act of 1808.[35]
It provided for the erection of asylums by authorities and fines
on overseers who neglected to send their dangerous lunatics to
such asylums. The building of asylums under this act was, however, permissive, so progress in its implementation was slow. By
1834 there were only about a dozen county asylums with, if
anything, a geographical bias towards the midlands and the
adjacent east coast.[36] With powers of compulsion in the background, overseers did take advantage of the new asylums while
continuing to use the older, charitable and private institutions
where these were more convenient. County asylums did not re-
strict admissions to persons resident in their own areas but could
and did take pauper patients from quite distant parishes.[37] During the early nineteenth century the provision of hospital facilities for lunatics increased and overseers made good use of them,
but by 1834 there were still many areas with inadequate facilities
and the cost of sending patients to the asylums continued to
discourage overseers from sending any but the most serious
cases.

Lunacy was a problem of individuals with their own peculiar
disabilities but overseers also had to deal with sickness in the
mass in the form of epidemics.[38] Since the medical profession
could offer little assistance in the way of cures the main task
was to alleviate suffering and deal with the problems raised by
widespread sickness. In the seventeenth century the great killer
was plague, of which the well-known outbreak of 1665 was not
the most serious, but the last major, epidemic. Its place was taken
in the eighteenth century by smallpox, to which was added in the
early nineteenth century the scourges of the new industrial towns:
typhoid and cholera. Plague was not only virtually incurable
and therefore highly lethal but it was very contagious and spread
easily and rapidly.[39] As a result the overseers were less concerned
with helping the sufferers than with coping with the economic
effects of measures taken to prevent the disease. On the local level
these involved preventing anyone going to or from a house

where the disease had struck. It fell to the overseers to support those who were prevented from working in this way. Similarly, at a wider level, strict precautions were taken to prevent anyone from a plague-ridden town or village entering one which was clear. Such measures hit those who were dependent for their livelihood on all branches of trade and commerce, since the movement of both new materials to manufacturers and finished goods to consumers was impeded. Towns which relied for their food on imports from adjacent villages suffered scarcity as well as a fall in purchasing power. Again, it was the duty of the poor law authorities to provide for those forced out of work by the general disruption of economic life and to co-operate with the magistrates in ensuring that scarce supplies were justly distributed. Though associated with disease, these were essentially administrative problems and in the many towns which were not dependent on one slump-prone industry, like textiles, epidemics of plague were the first occasions on which the overseers' resources were fully stretched. In this way plague contributed to the evolution of relief machinery by showing overseers what it was capable of if the need arose, and where it was in need of improvement.[40]

Smallpox presented similar problems but on a lesser scale. Since doctors could do more to cure those who contracted it and to prevent it spreading, it was thought sufficient to isolate the patients without cutting off and economically crippling whole communities. As a result the overseers could concentrate their attention on those who had actually contracted the disease. They had to arrange and pay for medical attention and organise isolation. In many parishes, even small villages, this was done by using some isolated house as a 'pest house', where infected persons could be sent to remain until the doctor certified their recovery.[41] After the mid-eighteenth century the centre of attention moved from cure to prevention, as first inoculation and later vaccination became available. Led by the larger towns many parishes, especially at first in the south, took advantage of these facilities, arranging for mass treatment of poor children and, less frequently, adults as well. The process was repeated from time to time to bring protection to each new generation.[42]

The new epidemics of the nineteenth century, typhoid and cholera, were closely associated with the new densely populated industrial towns. Like plague, they were ill-understood and in the absence of reliable cures the overseers' attention was concentrated on preventing the outbreak and spread of the disease. It was observed that these diseases were usually found in the most overcrowded and filthy sections of towns and thus the main feature of the prevention programme was a drive for cleanliness. The task of the overseers was to purchase cleaning materials, whitewash and the like and distribute them in the poor areas returning periodically to see that they had been used and that standards were maintained until the danger was past. When outbreaks occurred they were often dealt with in the same way that smallpox had been. The patients were removed to special hospitals acquired and fitted out in anticipation of the emergency where they could benefit from the limited skills of the medical profession.[43]

Epidemics were a minor aspect of the relief authorities' duties. They were few and far between and each disease presented a different set of problems whose solution was of limited value as a precedent in the next crisis. They are interesting because they reveal another aspect of the poor law's flexibility; the ability of its agencies to cope with a crisis, to push an organisation accustomed to gentle coasting into top gear to meet unusual and unexpected demands. The success or otherwise with which a parish coped with these emergencies can be a useful indication of its general efficiency.

In just over a century, medical relief had grown from the occasional payment of doctors' bills to a large and varied section of the relief system. What began as an economy measure to reduce the dependence of the sick poor, expanded to take in the whole range of the poor, and to bring within the range of the poor law others who had no claim for maintenance, but who could not afford the treatment they needed. Along with this expansion in availability went a significant diversification of the services. To the doctors' services were added those of midwives and nurses and then the institutions, infirmaries, dispensaries, asylums and so on became available. This expansion and diversification of poor relief represents one of the greatest achievements of the old poor law. It shows how the precepts of the 1601 Act could be exploited to discover new forms of need and new methods of relief and, by bringing the two together, create a vastly improved relief service.

These outlines are clear but much research is needed to fill in the detail. Individually outstanding documents such as contract agreements and quaint doctors' bills have been widely noticed but there has been little attempt to study medical relief in depth. The main source for this must be the overseers' accounts. They record expenditure in the various sectors—doctors, midwives, institutions—and place it in its wider context of poor relief as a whole. Another, somewhat neglected, source is the records of the institutions themselves. They give details of the subscriptions paid by the parishes, the accounts rendered to them and the relationship between parish and institution generally. By the detailed examination of these sources we could learn a good deal about the medical relief system, its growth and development, the spread of ideas from one area to another and its function, importance, and relative cost in the relief system as a whole.

Children

Generally the overseers were engaged in the short-term business of keeping their poor alive, and where possible restoring them to health, strength and independence. But a long-term view had to be taken with one group—the children.[44] Unless they were to remain paupers all their lives, steps had to be taken to ensure that, as they grew older, they would be able to become self supporting. This was recognised even in the Act of 1601, which was very general in most of its provisions, but laid down two specific policies to be pursued with respect to children. Firstly, if their parents could not support them, the overseers were obliged to set them to work so that they might contribute to their own maintenance. Secondly, they were to be put out as apprentices when they were old enough, so that they could be taught a useful craft. Taken with the general relief provisions of this act it can be said that these instructions covered the three responsibilities which the parish had to fulfil on behalf of children in its care. These were to support them, to give them work so that they could contribute towards that support and to provide training so that they might eventually support themselves.

Maintenance was the simplest task. If the children had parents who were sick, widowed, unemployed or otherwise pauperised, their keep was included in the family pension. If not, they were generally boarded out and their foster parents were paid a regular allowance.[45] Problems began to arise, however, when the parish found itself forced to stand in for those who had defaulted on their obligations to support their children. This situation usually arose in connection with illegitimacy; less frequently when wives and families had been deserted by their breadwinner. In either case the parish felt obliged to minimise its expenses by locating the father and taking steps to ensure that he fulfilled his duties. For this reason the relevant papers, warrants for arrest, affiliation orders, bonds for the maintenance of children and so on were accumulated in the parish records, and by their bulk tend to give the impression that a far greater proportion of the overseers' time and money was spent on these matters than was, in fact, the case. The work was onerous and resented because it concerned poverty which was preventable and often actually caused by immorality but its significance should not be exaggerated.[46]

Setting children to work was a far greater problem than maintenance and the obligation to do so was widely forgotten. The practical difficulties were considerable. The normal economic function of children was helping their parents in their employment and in many places there was no gainful activity to which children could be set outside the economic unit of the family. For this reason the various projects for the engagement of people to teach and employ children in textile and other crafts which do appear in the records from time to time were the exception rather than the rule. It was only in the large towns, where pauper children were fairly numerous, that it was really worth making permanent arrangements for the employment of children.[47] These usually involved the establishment of some sort of institution which can be regarded as a predecessor or an offshoot of the workhouse system which will be looked at in greater detail in the next chapter.[48]

The work provided for children had a secondary purpose of teaching them skills which would make them self supporting when they grew up, but the main vehicle for imparting such knowledge was apprenticeship as provided for in the 1601 Act.[49] Like illegitimacy, apprenticeship created a series of records of its own.[50] These have caused it to be emphasised out of all proportion to its significance and most of the comment has been hostile. Overseers have been criticised because they bound children to sweated or unskilled trades, placed them with masters outside the parish to give them a new settlement or used powers of compulsion to impose them on unwilling parishioners (they could not do both!). There is much evidence to support these allegations and if one examines the problems confronting the overseers it is not difficult to see why. Pauper children came from the lower strata of society and it would be quite unrealistic to expect the overseers to put them in a position to rise any higher. Equality of opportunity was unheard of either as a slogan or as a concept. It would have been thought quite unjust that a labouring man, who could offer his sons no better future than to follow in his footsteps, should contribute towards a rate fund which bought entry into more remunerative occupation for children dependent on the parish.

This attitude was reinforced by the economic facts of life. Many rural villages were dependent entirely on agriculture and the overseers had no option but to bind their boys to learn farming and their girls to learn domestic service. Village craftsmen might take apprentices from time to time but their capacity to do so was severely restricted by the static market which they served. If there was an industry in the village it was usually a branch of some domestic manufacture where the long-term prospects were no brighter than in agriculture.[51] In fact, it was in parishes of this type that overseers had most frequently to resort to the powers

granted in an Act of 1697 to compel ratepayers to take children
on a rota basis.[52] Parishes in or near towns had a wider range of
occupations to choose from but there were many others besides
overseers seeking good places for their children. The result was
that parish apprentices with limited funds behind them tended
to find themselves in the least attractive occupations. It might
also be added that they were perhaps the least attractive of apprentices. Among them were bastards, orphans and the products
of broken homes, and it is reasonable to assume that they suffered
in full measure from the emotional and psychological distur-
bances which we now know that these conditions produce. The
extent to which overseers found masters outside the parish with
the sole intention of giving the child a new settlement cannot be
assessed. What emerges very clearly from indentures and the
apprentice registers is the fact that they bound children to the
best occupation they could get whether in the parish or outside it.

Towards the end of the eighteenth century the problem of
finding masters was eased by the establishment of large textile
mills whose owners were willing to take large numbers of pauper
apprentices to attend their machinery. For a brief period this
opportunity was fully exploited by hard-pressed overseers not
only in parishes adjacent to the mills but also by those in the
metropolis and the rural south.[53] In so doing they went too far.
The abuse of sending young children so far from home and
family with no obligation for checking their subsequent welfare
was so outrageous that public opinion was aroused. Legislation
was passed to curtail the practice by insisting that proposed
bindings to distant parishes were scrutinised and approved by
magistrates and that a register of all bindings was kept in each
parish.[54] We cannot assess the impact of this significant example
of public opinion successfully bringing pressure to bear on the
legislature because we know so little about apprenticeship either
before or after. It is easy to find examples of children being sent
to the factories. Like so many of the abuses to which the poor
law administration was prone, they stand out because they caused
the creation of special documents, in this case correspondence
and agreements with factory owners. We know less about the

parishes which did not follow this policy and are quite unable to assess the proportion of pauper apprentices who went to factories.

Training poor children to earn their own living when they grew up was not confined to parish work schemes and apprenticeship. It also involved the provision of formal education, or at least, in the words of contemporaries, some instruction in 'reading, writing and casting accounts'. We find very few references to the education of outdoor poor but we know it was provided in workhouses and that it was often available to the poorest of independent labourers so it is reasonable to assume that schooling for the children was normally one of the many calls on the poor family's weekly pension.[55]

Dealing with poor children was one of the most important tasks of the poor relief authorities. It lacked glamour; there were no major innovations like the creation of workhouses, though children did use these; there was no massive expansion as in medical relief though some of this went to children. On the whole the relief of children was much the same in 1834 as it had been in 1601. The child received maintenance, with its own or a foster family, education to the standard available to his poorest independent contemporaries, opportunities for work and learning craft-skills and finally an apprenticeship. The importance of this work lay in its orientation towards the future. With the old and infirm the overseers simply had to provide maintenance until death. With the unemployed they did the same until work became available. But with children it was out of the question to support them until they died and they could not be expected to work without proper training. The children therefore presented overseers with one of their best opportunities for constructive work. In this light we can see that much of the work which has been done on the poor children fails to penetrate deep enough. It is inadequate merely to describe what was done, we must try to establish whether there was any clear policy or whether it was just a matter of dealing with each case as it came up. To understand the position in a particular parish we must have a clearer general background. We need to know how many parishes provided education, craft training, or sweated dead-end employment and how many sent apprentices to the mills. Were there any geographical variations in attitudes to these policies or changes through time? Finally we must discover what these policies achieved. This will require investigation in the places whither the children were sent as well as whence they came. Not until such investigations have been carried out shall we be able to say how overseers tackled the problem of poor children and whether they were successful in their efforts.

Notes to this chapter are on pages 130–4

Chapter 5

Institutional Relief

The Evolution of the Workhouse Movement

To many people, casting their minds back to the days before the modern welfare state or recollecting the words of Dickens, the workhouse is synonymous with the poor law. In fact they are thinking of a later period than that under consideration here but the new poor law grew out of the old; the workhouse became ubiquitous under an administration which sought to universalise what it thought was best in the system which it superseded. Their influence on the future alone, makes methods of institutional relief devised and developed by the local poor law authorities in the two centuries before 1834 a subject worthy of examination.[1]

This influence on the future was not limited to inspiring the central feature of poor relief in the nineteenth century. The old poor law workhouses can be seen as the ancestor of most of the institutions which form part of the modern social services. They were used as old people's homes, occupational training centres, maternity, mental and general hospitals, childrens' homes and hostels for the homeless. With their workshops, schools and sick wards they constituted the full range of welfare services in microcosm from which the modern specialised institutions have grown. A movement which was seeking to achieve so much is also worthy of study for itself and not merely for its progeny. In this section and the next we shall look at the way in which the workhouse system evolved, the forces making for its creation and the way in which it came to encompass the various functions mentioned above. We shall then look at the problems faced by the administrators seeking to achieve these ends, noting not only the successes but the disasters which exemplify failure to over-come the obstacles. It is important to recognise how great these obstacles were, for it is only against this background that we can assess the achievement of the workhouse authorities. The estab-lishment of an institution was a new venture for most parishes, bringing with it unprecedented responsibilities. They might be used to looking after public buildings, the parish church, alms-houses and charity endowments and to handling considerable sums of money, collected from the ratepayers and handed out to the poor in cash, but the management of a community was something new. It involved spending on goods and services, getting value for money and keeping detailed accounts. It meant organising the inmates to do the cooking and cleaning and to produce saleable goods. These were a whole range of new activi-ties. On the efficiency with which they were executed depended the kind of conditions in which the paupers lived; their physical environment and the activities which made up their daily routine.

The poor law evolved to fill the gap between the endowed charities on the one hand and the vagrancy laws on the other. It was responsible for the maintenance of those for whom the limited charitable funds were insufficient but who had not actually committed an offence. Both sectors had their institutions, alms-houses and houses of correction, and it is hardly surprising that the poor law authorities should have followed this example when seeking to provide for the people under their care.

The earliest evidence of distinctive poor law institutions is from the 1630s when several parishes, chiefly in textile towns, reported to the privy council that they had established work-houses where their unemployed could be given supervised em-ployment.[2] We do not know much of these institutions or how long they lasted but occasional chance references show that workhouses were to be found here and there throughout the seventeenth century. Our sources are sparse and there may well have been more than we suspect.[3]

The modern workhouse movement is always said to have begun in 1696 when Bristol obtained a local act to govern poor law administration in the town.[4] The example was quickly followed by Crediton, Tiverton, Exeter, Hereford, Colchester, Hull and Shaftesbury in 1698, King's Lynn and Sudbury in 1700, Gloucester in 1702, Plymouth in 1708 and Norwich in 1712. Other towns and parishes applied to parliament without success.[5] The workhouse was not the only, or indeed the main, theme of these acts and it is probable that many of the towns were already using institutions.[6] The acts were designed to regulate the constitutional and administrative structures but by enshrining the existence of the workhouse in a statute they made it a central and permanent branch of poor relief.

It is just as the first rush of local acts is diminishing that we find more evidence of workhouses in smaller towns and in villages.[7] It seems unlikely that the local act movement had much influence on these rural experiments. Most of the local act towns were in the south-west, conveniently situated to study and emulate the Bristol scheme; only one is in the Home Counties area where most of the workhouses reported in the period 1710–22 were located. In considering evidence that workhouses were more numerous in this period we must bear in mind that our sources are also more plentiful. Even so, it does seem that the obscure workhouse movement of the seventeenth century was gathering momentum in the years before 1722. In that year workhouses were at last given a formal place in the poor law by means of an act which legalised what had long existed with neither the permission nor the prohibition of the law.

A workhouse could be justified under the 1601 provision for setting the poor to work but the absence of any positive legal permission may well have deterred parishes from taking this step. With no clear authority to spend public money in this way it was open to minorities to frustrate the will of the majority by obstructing the foundation and impeding the progress of a workhouse by questioning the legality of every step. Such difficulties were probably rare but this statute of 1722 removed them with three simple enactments:

F

(i) Parishes or groups of parishes (nothing was said about how such unions should be formed or about how the relations between their members should be regulated) might obtain (by purchase, building or renting) premises for use as a workhouse.

(ii) Parishes or unions of parishes might contract with someone to manage their workhouse. The vague wording of this clause meant that it could apply not only to contractors for a lump sum but also to salaried governors.

(iii) Relief could be denied to those who refused to enter the workhouse. By applying this 'workhouse test' overseers could seek to eliminate the idle from their books and overrule magistrates who ordered payments to undeserving cases.[8]

Apart from an amendment in 1795[9] enabling magistrates to grant outdoor relief in cases of temporary need, in spite of the workhouse test, this act remained in full force to the end of the old poor law period.

The only major piece of general workhouse legislation between 1722 and 1834 was Gilbert's Act, passed in 1782.[10] In a sense it was the tip of an iceberg, being the only one of numerous bills promoting analogous schemes to pass the scrutiny of parliament. Its advantage over the others was that it was an enabling act; it did not impose expenditure on the local authorities. Even its author admitted that it was a watered-down version of what he really wanted. He thought an emasculated reform was better than no reform at all and continued the battle for a nationwide compulsory scheme.[11] In its provisions Gilbert's Act gave the smaller parishes and groups of parishes the clearly defined administrative and constitutional structures enjoyed in local act towns. Not a great deal was said about the workhouse itself but its inmates were only to be 'such as are become indigent by old age, sickness or infirmities' and poor children accompanied, where necessary, by their mothers. A set of rules to be observed in workhouses established under this act was published with it as a schedule.

Such then was the limited legal framework within which parishes seeking to establish and operate workhouses were obliged to work during the second half of the old poor law period. If they were wealthy and ambitious enough they could apply for a local act. Otherwise they had to choose between the vague terms of the 1722 Act or the closley circumscribed Gilbert blueprint. The main source of information about how the workhouse movement developed in the century after 1722 are the returns which parliament obtained from every parish in 1776, 1804 and 1815.[12] This material must be handled with care and used to give a general impression rather than precise statistics. Unfortunately no direct comparisons are possible because the information sought was different on each occasion. In 1776 parishes were asked to state how many workhouses they had and how many persons they could accommodate. This can produce misleading information in the case of union workhouses where one may find each member of the union returning the workhouse which they shared. On the other hand, most of the parishes in a union might send in a *nil* return, leaving the workhouse to be claimed by the parish in which it was actually situated.[13] The 1804 returns give the number of people in the workhouse and the 1815 returns record this figure less the children of adult inmates. Such returns reflect not only the use made of workhouses in various parts of the country but also the different types of workhouse organisation. They reveal a marked contrast between those districts where each workhouse served one parish and those areas where union workhouses predominated. In the latter nearly every parish supported one or two inmates and even those parishes which reported none were probably members of a union.

For the period between 1722 and 1776 we must rely however on the same sources as for the earlier period: the increasingly abundant parochial records and chance references in print. The 1720s are particularly well documented in the two editions of *An Account of Several Workhouses*.[14] This pamphlet is far from comprehensive but does emphasise the momentum gained by the movement after 1722. For the years between the returns and after 1815 we must rely on the same sources, augmented in the latter case by the information collected by the Royal Commission of 1832. Our sources may be patchy and in places unreliable but they are sufficient for the construction of a skeleton to which the flesh may be added when more research has been completed.

One fact which stands out from the mass of uncertainty is the leading part which the towns played in the workhouse movement. We have seen that it was the towns which established the first experimental workhouses in the 1630s, kept the movement alive in the later seventeenth century, and introduced and exploited the local act procedure. Many of those which were still without a workhouse were among the first to exploit the powers granted by the 1722 Act.[15] There can be little doubt that by the middle of the eighteenth century the urban community of market town size or above, which had no workhouse, was a rarity. Not only had almost every town a workhouse; but the workhouses were retained over long periods, very often continuously from their foundation until the demise of the old poor law. The legal and administrative provisions relating to urban workhouses varied widely. Towns and metropolitan parishes continued to use the local act procedure and there was a steady stream of enactments, some breaking new ground, and some amendments to earlier acts. Many of these acts provided for the union of parishes, for nowhere was this more desirable than in the ancient boroughs where numerous tiny parishes were grouped within a single community. In other towns unions were achieved under the 1722 Act[16] and later Gilbert's Act was sometimes adopted to revitalise an ailing workhouse administration.[17] Such unions might serve all or only some of the parishes in a town, while in others there might be several single parish workhouses or a combination of union and single parish workhouses.[18]

Towns led the way not only in the establishment of workhouses and the creation of unions but in the construction of purpose-built workhouses. This became quite common from about 1760 onwards when many growing towns were forced by pressure of numbers to replace their existing buildings and chose to do it in this way.[19] In contrast to the towns our picture of workhouse organisation in the rural areas is much less clear and far more complex. In the greater part of England and Wales each parish preferred to have its own institution. Most were tiny and many were short-lived. Authorities founded them with high hopes of a reduction in rates but discovered after a few years that the overheads outweighed any savings gained from the workhouse test. Thus we find different parishes reporting workhouses in each of the parliamentary returns and some having two or three during a period of a century, reverting to outdoor relief in the intervening years.[20] We know so little about these small short-lived workhouses that it is impossible to say whether there were any long-term trends towards increasing or declining popularity of workhouses. The workhouse movement only thrived in rural areas if parishes joined together in unions to give their institutions a financial base similar to that enjoyed by their urban counterparts. We know very little about the growth of the union workhouse movement during the eighteenth century but it is clear that by 1800 two districts were well provided with union workhouses and that the idea had been tried, with varying success in many other areas.[21]

The main stronghold of the workhouse unions was the northern industrial belt: Lancashire, Cheshire, Derbyshire, Nottinghamshire and the West Riding.[22] By 1800 there was a network of union workhouses in all these counties but how long it had been there we do not know. Several unions had been founded in south-west Lancashire before 1740 but it is not yet clear whether the idea spread thence to the other counties or arose spontaneously in various parts of the region. What is certain is that the rural union idea was spreading outwards from this area in the early nineteenth century. The provisions of Gilbert's Act were used to replace the older unions in Derbyshire and Nottinghamshire and to form new ones in Staffordshire, Leicestershire, Warwickshire, Lincolnshire, east and north Yorkshire, Westmorland and north Lancashire.[23]

The other centre of rural unions was East Anglia where eight unions were formed in the years 1764–6. They were unique in that this was the only occasion on which rural parishes followed the urban precedent of obtaining a local act to create a formal incorporation. In this way the unions were made permanent and their constitutional and administrative procedures were firmly laid down.[24] This gave them a considerable advantage over unions formed under the 1722 Act. Although some of the latter proved to be remarkably stable and lasted with much the same membership for over a century, others were more short-lived and their financial arrangements could be thrown badly out of joint when parishes exercised their powers to leave and join another union with excessive frequency.[25] As their membership was firmly laid down by parliament the East Anglian unions were untroubled by such difficulties. The number of unions in this area was increased later in the century when several Gilbert Unions came into being.[26] From time to time examples have been found of workhouse unions formed in other parts of the country during the eighteenth century and it is probable that more remain to be discovered. It appears that these were relatively isolated unions or groups of unions and they did not lead to the idea taking hold on the extensive scale found in the northern counties. On the other hand in certain southern districts just as much as in the north, Gilbert's Act served as a basis for the formation of new unions during the early nineteenth century. There were several in the south coast counties from Kent to Hampshire and isolated examples occur elsewhere.[27]

Before drawing together the various strands which make up the history of the workhouse movement in this period we must remind ourselves that the picture is likely to be biased by the greater abundance of our sources for more recent periods. This factor is likely to lead us to the impression that workhouse activity was increasing steadily, even if it was not. Having given due weight to this factor it does seem fair to say that the workhouse movement was steadily growing and developing although we cannot measure the rate of progress and there may well have been temporary relapses of which we know nothing. The major milestones are clear: the false start in the 1630s, the bursts of activity following the first use of the local act procedure and leading up to, and ensuing from, the 1722 Act, and finally the belated implementation of Gilbert's Act in the early nineteenth century. We cannot say for sure that there were more workhouses in towns or more parishes in unions in 1834 than fifty or a hundred years before, but there were certainly more purpose-built institutions and progress implies improvements in standards as well as numerical expansion. Our data may be insufficient to support a reliable quantification of the expansion and improvement of workhouse provision but we can seek to understand these phenomena by examining the objectives of the poor law authorities which sponsored them.

Workhouse Objectives

Workhouse objectives are made clear in the records created by those responsible for workhouse administration, which fall into two groups (a) those relating to the internal management of the house and (b) those dealing with the relationship between the workhouse and the parish. Neither class has survived in abundance, the former being rarer than the latter for reasons not far to seek.

The internal records were a matter for the person appointed to manage the institution. A contractor was often answerable to nobody and if he kept any records at all they needed only to be the minimum for his own purposes. Governors were not so free. They often had to produce accounts for audit by the ratepayers and these were essential in union houses where the expenses had to be apportioned among the parishes. Even so, there was frequently nothing to prevent them taking the books with them when they left. Another reason for the disappearance of work house records is the fact that when these institutions were closed, either through a change in parish policy or when the boards of guardians were established, they had no successors to take the records and there was no legal obligation to save them. This made the internal records of workhouses very vulnerable to destruction and it has meant that a significant proportion of those which have come down to us are from institutions taken over by

the guardians. Their successors have provided continuous cus-
tody ever since. The internal records of workhouses fall into
two classes, financial and personal. At their best the former give
a detailed account of the types and quality of food, materials and
equipment being bought and can give the student a detailed
insight into the day-to-day operation of the workhouse. This can
be complemented by the information in the personal records
which range from detailed admissions registers to brief statements of the numbers in the house and can give an indication of
the sort of people who were admitted, how long they stayed and
so on.

The records of the relationship between the parish and workhouse are more abundant but less valuable. Many of them are
of a formal nature, agreements with masters, rules of management, terms of unions and such items. They show the structural
arrangements and the aspirations of those who made them but
tell us little of what went on inside the workhouse itself. More
valuable, in the rare cases where they have survived, are the
minute books of parish or union committees of management
which record the outlines of policy developments. In the case of
union workhouses another valuable source is the regular bills
they sent out to the parishes which, after payment, found their
way into the bundles of overseers' vouchers. They vary greatly
in form and content. Some are brief statements of the sum due
while others are on sophisticated printed forms. Most are somewhere between these extremes. They generally indicate the cost
of keeping a person in the workhouse over a period of time;
when names are given it may be possible to discover which kinds
of poor were dealt with in this way and how long individuals
remained in the workhouse.

These records rarely give information regarding the motives
for establishing a workhouse or for running it in a particular way.
Generally this is something the historian must work out for
himself, taking the evidence of what was actually done and seeking to identify the pattern and threads of policy underlying it.

One objective which was usually made clear in the records
was the application of the workhouse test, which had been given

statutory sanction in the 1722 Act.[28] This was clearly a dominant factor in the minds of many of those who established workhouses in immediate response to this legislation. Whether we find an order in the minutes stipulating that all who refused to enter the new workhouse should lose their relief, or notice that the pension list disappears from the accounts after its completion, the conclusion is clear. Similar phenomena can be found in the records throughout our period both in parishes establishing a new workhouse and in those reforming or introducing a new policy into an old one. The continued resort to the workhouse test shows continuing confidence in its efficacy to reduce an inflated rate-burden, but the fact that parishes had to reintroduce it from time to time indicates that at intervals a less rigid policy had been pursued. This sort of change is more difficult to trace. We can see it happening as the pension list reappears in the accounts or outdoor relief is occasionally granted by the vestry. But what were the reasons behind this change of policy? Was it simply that the workhouse was full up or had the authorities recognised that the workhouse was more suitable for some kinds of poor than for others?

The most useful information on this subject is to be found in the admissions registers and lists of inmates, but vestry minutes and monthly accounts presented to parishes in workhouse unions can be useful. There is also a good deal of information, of uneven quality, in Eden's appendix of parochial reports[29] and in Appendix B of the 1834 Royal Commission report.[30] Naturally no two workhouses had exactly the same approach and few pursued the same policy throughout the period of their existence. Nevertheless a certain similarity of approach can be detected. Its essence was a tendency for the workhouse to become a receptacle for the most long-term and difficult cases: orphans, young mothers—deserted, widowed and unmarried—with one or two children, those with permanent infirmities both mental and physical, and those among the aged who were either solitary and homeless or in need of care and attention from others.

To see why this pattern should have emerged we must consider the various factors which overseers had to take into account

when selecting paupers for institutional relief. In this as in all
else they were torn between the conflicting claims of economy
and adequate standards of relief. All other considerations were
overshadowed by the fact that overheads made the workhouse
more expensive than outdoor relief. There had therefore to be
some compensating factor before a case became eligible for institutional relief. Such factors included the economy of using
other inmates to nurse and care for the sick and bed-ridden poor
in the workhouse rather than in their own homes, the saving in
the high cost of providing other accommodation for solitaries and
small families and the benefit of exacting a small work contribution from enfeebled but not incapacitated paupers. Working
against these crude economic calculations was the unwillingness
of many officers to disturb the home life of couples and families
whose poverty was no fault of their own. One can see that these
factors would apply with varying force to different classes of
pauper. In the case of the elderly, the arguments clearly cut both
ways. While they could look after themselves and perhaps cultivate a garden or do a little work at harvest time there was everything to be said for leaving them in the familiar surroundings
of the cottage. On the other hand, if they had lost the help of
their spouses or if failing health and strength made them dependent upon the aid of others, there was much to be said for
taking them into the house where nursing facilities and domestic
help were available.

The inmates lists show young deserted, unmarried and
widowed mothers as the largest able-bodied group in most workhouses and there were very good reasons for bringing them in
when they had small families. If they had no more than a couple
of children, outdoor accommodation was likely to be costly and
the woman's time used inefficiently because the need to care for
the child would keep her from work. In the workhouse a few
could look after the children while the remainder were set on
useful tasks. In any case, nobody had any qualms about forcing
unmarried mothers, whose plight aroused hostility rather than
sympathy, into the workhouse. The attitude to widows and deserted mothers with large families was rather different. Where a

mother was fully occupied with a family and had older children
perhaps able to work, the authorities' natural unwillingness to
break up the home was reinforced by economic factors.

In the rare event of orphans becoming dependent upon the
parish it was necessary to provide not only housing and maintenance but adult care and support *in loco parentis*. This was
normally achieved by boarding out, but where there was a workhouse, its facilities for nursing, schooling and occupational training, already provided for other poor children, could be extended
to those without parents. The workhouse, with its facilities for
nursing and domestic help, was well adapted to housing the sick
poor. Of course if the patient was a member of a family, and
especially if his infirmity was likely to be temporary, there was
everything to be said for leaving him in the care of his relations,
the parish helping with monetary relief. But if he had no family
or, as was often the case with lunatics, was unfit to remain in the
home, there was a clear-cut case for workhouse relief. Having a
workhouse to hand meant that the authorities could use it for
various contingencies which might arise such as the housing of
families returned under removal orders, until more permanent
arrangements could be made, and as a maternity ward for the
unmarried mother who had nowhere to go to have her baby even
if she could leave the house after the birth and support it from
her earnings and its paternal contribution.

Able-bodied males rarely found their way into the workhouse.
Where the workhouse test was in operation there might be the
odd one or two for whom the prospect of the workhouse was not
deterrent enough. For the able-bodied in genuine need the workhouse offered no solution since, as a rule, such poverty was temporary whether caused by unemployment between jobs, sickness,
or worklessness following a downward turn in the trade cycle.
Taking people into the workhouse under such circumstances
could be positively counter-productive, breaking up the home,
disrupting normal life and making it more difficult to start again
when work appeared. In the case of cyclical unemployment the
sheer impracticability of workhouse relief made these other objec-
tions look trivial. It is true that in the early seventeenth century,

when mass poverty was to be found in many textile towns, working houses were set up to deal with it. Some were in the form of non-residential factories rather than true workhouses. Their success was limited because, as was realised in the early nineteenth century when this type of problem again became serious, there was little to be gained by putting the unemployed to work on the very jobs from which private enterprise had laid them off as being unprofitable. Inevitably such institutions died with the emergency which had created them.[31]

This picture of the able-bodied poor as rarely entering the workhouse but receiving doles and pensions to tide them over periods of temporary necessity contrasts sharply with the system of relief projected by many of the eighteenth-century pamphleteers. Their greatest concern was the way in which, allegedly, the rates were being squandered on idle malingerers and scroungers. Their view was no doubt biased by their residence in towns especially the metropolis, which attracted like pins to a magnet all those seeking an easy or dubious mode of life. Consequently their writings are full of plans for large well-administered workhouses serving groups of parishes, hundreds or even counties in which the idle masses could be set to work. Some optimistic writers envisaged such institutions not only paying their way but even earning a surplus to support the deserving poor and allow the rates to be abolished.[32] No contrast could be greater than that between the theorists' dreams and what we actually find, even in the best run workhouses. They were homes for the most needy of the deserving poor; the children, the sick, the insane and the elderly, those with no homes of their own and no relatives to nurse and care for them. The application of the workhouse test required facilities for work, which were used for training the young and by those not totally incapacitated. But, in spite of the name, most workhouses were more like hospitals, boarding schools and old peoples' homes than factories.

Conditions in the Workhouse

No aspect of old poor law workhouses is as badly documented as the question of what conditions were like inside them. We have ample record of the daily routines to which overseers and vestries aspired and numerous descriptions of their most abject failures, but very little record of the conditions in which the poor lived or of their daily lives in the ordinary run-of-the-mill workhouse, outstanding neither for its squalor and indiscipline nor for its exemplary efficiency. As far as the daily routine is concerned we are dependent almost entirely upon statements of aspirations made by the authorities in the form of codes of rules for the internal management of their workhouses.[33] Many of them have survived and they are much alike. The differences were in detail and, more important, in execution. The main features of these codes can be summarised briefly with examples taken from the relatively full set of rules made at Loughborough in 1770. To minimise expenditure on lighting and heating and make full use of daylight most workhouses had different routines in winter and in summer. At Loughborough, in summer 'strong people' rose at 6am and retired at 9pm; in winter, their hours were from 8am to 8pm. Usually the first task of the day was cleaning the rooms which, at Loughborough, meant having the beds made by 9am and the rooms swept and cleaned by 10am. In addition the bedrooms had to be washed twice a week in summer and once a week in winter. The kitchen, dining and other communal rooms were to be swept or washed everyday and the cooking and eating utensils cleaned after every meal. Generally the rules also stressed the need for personal hygiene. The thorough cleansing of new admissions which received so much emphasis at Hull was by no means unusual. At Loughborough the master and mistress were instructed to set a good example in this respect, to see that it was followed, and to instruct the children in personal cleanliness. Having completed the early morning cleaning, partaken of breakfast and perhaps attended morning prayers the inmates dispersed to their routine daily tasks—the work that gave their institution its name.

As we have seen, in workhouses the feeble in mind and body were in a majority and there were very few who could have made a living outside. Indeed, the object of the ubiquitous workhouse test was to ensure that they left as soon as they could do so. Among the typical workhouse population the best able to put in a full days work were the younger women: the widows and unmarried mothers. Naturally the domestic chores of the house made the first call on their time. These included the cooking, cleaning and washing, the nursing of the elderly and sick, the supervision of the children. If there were time to spare, they repaired and made clothes for the inmates and, as sometimes happened, for the outdoor poor as well. The men of the house, even if elderly or in poor health could often do a little work, though perhaps not a full day. They were the main source of labour for remunerative employment but they too had their domestic duties, heaving coal, chopping wood and the like which had to come first.

What sort of work was provided in the workhouses? The most widespread was textile working, spinning for the women, winding for the children and weaving for the men. In towns with a local industrial speciality this would find its way into the workhouse as being the one thing which the poor and the authorities knew about. In some workhouses old men who had been craftsmen were able to continue their trades (eg tailoring, shoemaking) as far as their reduced strength would allow and perhaps impart their skills to the younger inmates. One occupation which became something of a workhouse speciality was oakum picking. Tedious but not physically demanding it was the ideal way of deterring the able-bodied while providing a productive occupation for the unskilled and enfeebled deserving poor. Some workhouses used their labour force to save money rather than to earn it. Many had land where the inmates could keep pigs, cultivate a kitchen garden and in exceptional cases graze a herd of cows. Remunerative work, in theory the main function of the workhouse, was in practice of limited importance. Facilities for employment were needed when it became necessary to employ the workhouse test, and to enable those inmates who could to make a contribution to the cost of their maintenance, but the paltry level of paupers' earnings made a mockery of the pamphleteers' grandiose schemes for self-supporting workhouses. In fact it is probable that the poor law system gained more from the improved standards of relief obtained by the use of pauper labour to care for the aged and sick than it did from cash earned by the poor.[34]

The daily routine of the children in the workhouse was often more varied than that of their elders. Naturally the youngest of them were among the unproductive inmates to whom the able-bodied women had to give time and attention. When they reached the age of fourteen or sixteen years the children were able to support themselves and were sent out to apprenticeships or into domestic service. The time of the intervening age group was more valuable than that of any other group in the house because it had to be used to educate and train the children so that when they left they could obtain a good situation and be placed on the road to independent adulthood. The two main elements in their training were the imparting of information likely to be of use in the future and training in habits of disciplined regular work. In all but the smallest workhouses the transmission of information included some kind of formal schooling.[35] The quality and content of such education must have varied enormously, depending on the amount of time given to it and the standard of teaching. As the children grew older, it was usual for them to spend more time working, although it was rare for any special provision to be made for them. Helping with the domestic work of the house and learning the ubiquitous textile trade, the local handicraft or a trade practised by some elderly inmate was thought adequate vocational training for those who could not expect to occupy any but the lowest rungs of the economic ladder. Some authorities of which Loughborough was one arranged schemes of work for workhouse girls which were related to the types of employment they were expected to enter. Those 'able and fit for service' were to learn stocking knitting and wool and flax spinning 'towards providing clothing for the people in the house' while those with 'bodily infirmities' and therefore unsuitable for service were to learn soft work spinning so as to have a reasonable chance of earning a living outside when grown up. At the other extreme were workhouses like Manchester with its much criticised pin manufactory where the primary consideration was profitable employment, and short-term remuneration was placed above the long-term needs of the children.[36]

Sunday was the one day when the regular routine was broken, at least for the inmates not engaged on essential kitchen duties. Two visits to the local church or chapel—the concession to nonconformists was almost universal—were generally the order of the day and the remaining time was often filled with Bible-reading and the like.

Most sets of rules specified mealtimes but said nothing about the food. Other local records are similarly silent on this subject[37] but the deficiency is made good by the numerous dietaries printed by Eden.[38] They are interesting because of the regional variations which they reveal. There is a marked contrast between the frequent use of potatoes in many northern parishes and the prominent place given to bread and cheese in the south. Such differences probably tell us more about local working-class eating habits than they do about diverse administrative policies. While we know a good deal about the kind of food which was eaten we know very little about the quantity. Much of the evidence is of a speculative or suspect nature. In theory the forces making for underfeeding were considerable. Contractors seeking to support the poor and make a profit out of a lump sum had a positive incentive to skimp the food while governors, overseers and vestries were under constant pressure to keep the rates down. In spite of this workhouses were often criticised for overfeeding and for making life within their doors more attractive than an independent existence outside.[39] Naturally the Royal Commission of 1832 was especially interested in abuses of this kind and it collected examples in order to demonstrate the contrast between the existing system and the new order which it proposed. Some parishes permitted deviations from the fixed dietary. These usually applied to the most deserving poor; special foods and sometimes wine for the sick and little extras for the elderly, usually tobacco for the men and tea and sugar for the women.

Turning from the administrative to the physical environment in which the workhouse inmates lived we are, if anything, even more short of factual information. Our main evidence is, of course, the buildings themselves. Since many of them were quite old in 1834 it is hardly surprising that few remain for us to study. This is particularly true in the case of towns. Increasing populations made them inadequate for poor law purposes at an early date and their city-centre sites have made them natural targets for the redevelopers' bulldozers. On the other hand town workhouses which have survived can usually be located fairly easily because large-scale town maps were commonplace by the early nineteenth century. Having found the building it is simply a matter of determining which parts of the existing structure were there in 1834. Rural parish workhouses are more likely to have survived but are more difficult to locate. As often as not they were converted farmhouses or rows of cottages which could easily revert to their former use when, as happened over much of southern England shortly after 1834, the poor were transferred to a brand new union workhouse. Maps of villages and market towns are more scarce and do not always mark workhouses as such. The poor law archaeologist is therefore forced to resort to the less reliable sources of a chance find in an unrelated document and the local folk memory.

The workhouse buildings which have survived in the greatest number are those which were large enough to be taken over by the new unions. They were generally purpose-built institutions erected by rural unions or market towns in the early nineteenth century.[40] As such they are hardly a representative sample but it is a tribute to the overseers and vestry men who designed and erected them that some are still in use today as hospitals and old peoples' homes. The building alone can tell us very little but considered in conjunction with its human and physical contents it can present a clear picture of pauper life in the old poor law period. By bringing together lists of inmates and room by room

G

inventories[41] and relating them to the building itself we can re-construct the environment which a local authority provided for its poor. The shortage of records and buildings means that oppor-tunities to do this will be rare and in fact an analysis of this nature remains to be carried out.

In the absence of detailed information of this sort we can only outline some of the main features of workhouse building. In the first flush of eighteenth-century enthusiasm for workhouses, purpose-built structures were rare except in the local act towns. Parishes acting under the terms of the 1722 Act usually bought or rented and converted a farmhouse, town house or row of cottages, or put a property already in public ownership as a charity endowment to this public use.[42] From the late eighteenth century onwards newly formed rural unions and market towns needing more workhouse accommodation to cope with their grow-ing populations erected purpose-built structures.[43] Their main advantage in comparison with converted buildings was the com-munal rooms which were made large enough for the working and eating requirements of their large families. It is probable that overcrowding was only a problem in towns where the population was increasing rapidly. Elsewhere workhouses were often work-ing below capacity because they had been built to take the whole of the parish poor and had become emptier as a more flexible and realistic policy was adopted.

So much then for the background—the people selected for workhouse relief and the buildings and furniture which sur-rounded them. The crucial question was whether the ratepayers and their officers could so organise these people and materials to create a harmonious and efficient community, ministering to its own wants and perhaps contributing a little towards the cost of its upkeep or whether they would find it degenerating into squalid and undisciplined chaos. Ultimately a workhouse stood or fell by its owners' ability to solve the managerial problem.

The simplest solution was for the ratepayers, through the officers or an elected committee, to do the job themselves.[44] This involved procuring provisions, organising duty rotas and ensur-ing that they were carried out. The weakness of this arrangement was that it imposed too great a burden on the people involved. To run smoothly, a workhouse needed constant supervision and regular attention to the dull routine, which men with their own affairs to attend to were unwilling or unable to give. The result was that the work fell to the dedicated few or was simply neglected. Ultimately pressure would grow for a full-time administrator to be appointed.

In implementing such a policy the parish faced three main problems. The first was the selection of an individual or couple to undertake the task. There were various approaches. In early times especially there was a tendency to seek specialists. Towns often thought in terms of work and employed manufacturing specialists. In villages the job was thought of more in housekeeping terms and a widow with appropriate experience might be preferred. Whatever their preferences it is clear that, when it came to the point, parishes had to take whoever would do the work for the money offered. Inevitably many of those selected were deficient in character, principle, competence or even all three. As a result relationships were often embittered and vestries found themselves constantly striving to keep their servants up to the mark or seeking replacements who could do better. It was on this point that many of the short-lived rural workhouses must have failed. If all the vestry wanted was a residential institution with a woman little better than a pauper herself in charge well and good, but if they wanted the inmates organised for productive as well as domestic labour they simply could not hire the administrative skills they required at the price they could afford. Larger workhouses with more funds at their disposal were able to appeal to a wider range of prospective governors and the extensive paperwork involved often made these posts appeal to persons with clerical experience. Such individuals often adapted themselves well to the administrative duties of workhouse management and gave their employers a period of stable efficiency which contrasted markedly with the constant experimentation which characterised the search for a really effective manager.

The second problem was to fix the precise terms of employment. Many agreements between parishes or unions and their

governors have come down to us. They are typical of many poor
law documents in that they vary from a scrappy entry in a
minute book to a formal parchment indenture. Towns produced
more formal agreements than rural parishes; these documents
became more complex as time passed and as the parishes learned
by experience of more points which had to be settled in advance,
and in writing. The content of these agreements varied greatly
in detail but there were two main types, the lump sum contract[45]
and the salary and expenses system.[46] Here as in other branches
of poor relief the contract had the advantage of simplicity and
apparent economy and also suffered from the same defects. By
employing a salaried governor the parish entered a more open-
ended commitment (which is what an obligation to relieve the
poor is) but was able to control more precisely how much was
spent on the various aspects of workhouse relief. Naturally, both
types of agreement could include other duties besides workhouse management. Relieving poor, collecting rates, clerical work
and keeping accounts might be added to the governor's duties.
We know little of the distribution of the two systems. A curious
development of the contract system whereby the contractor took
the poor, from whatever parishes chose to employ him, into his
own house, seems to have been a purely metropolitan phenomenon but the other two systems overlapped considerably.
There is some evidence that, as with medical relief, the contract
was more favoured in the south than the north. Without more
research, which must be extensive, systematic and detailed, we
cannot be sure. It should be possible, however, to establish
regional patterns, trends through time, and the extent to which
parishes learned from their own and their neighbours' experience.

The third problem was how the ratepayers were to exercise
control over their servant, the contractor or salaried governor.
We have already seen that ratepayers were averse to giving up
time to supervise the details of workhouse affairs, yet the need
to control their employees required that they did so to a greater
or lesser extent. The result was that in many parishes the supervision was minimal, depending entirely on the annual audit of
accounts. Elsewhere, often after the discovery of fraud or mal-

administration, the ratepayers appointed committees to supervise the work of the governor in varying degrees of detail.

One factor was present to aggravate all three problems. It was the absence on any significant scale of a body of knowledge and experience about workhouse management. True, each parish had its own past experience to draw upon, but this had first to be painfully acquired. But we know that vestries contemplating the establishment or reform of a workhouse visited or sought information about institutions in neighbouring parishes[47] and that a few individuals became career workhouse managers bringing their experience, over a lifetime, to the service of several parishes.[48] Even so, each step forward had to be worked out by each authority in the context of its own circumstances. When one considers the administrative problems and practical difficulties facing so many parishes one is impressed less by the many abuses which arose than by the considerable progress and improvement which was achieved.

Notes to this chapter are on pages 134–8

Chapter 6

The Able-bodied Poor

The Traditional Approach

The main achievement of the old poor law was, as we have seen, the establishment of an effective, comprehensive and flexible system for the relief of the deserving poor—the aged, the sick, one-parent families and so on. Yet this task was only peripheral to what, in 1601 was thought to be its main purpose: to solve the problem of unemployment and its consequential evils by setting the able-bodied poor to work. To be effective this policy required curbs to be placed on begging which necessitated provision for those who had deservedly obtained their sustenance in this way. Two centuries or so later the failure of the old poor law to deal adequately with the able-bodied poor of the industrial revolution led to its being substantially amended. Thus, the able-bodied poor may have been peripheral to the main activities of the old poor law, but they played a very significant part in the evolution of its legislative framework. It is therefore essential to examine the way in which the parochial authorities tackled the problems of able-bodied poverty.

In discussing the classification of various kinds of poverty, we found that the variety of human situations made this difficult, and to classify the able-bodied was the most difficult task of all. It is possible to distinguish between the unemployed and the underemployed, individual poverty and mass poverty, long-term poverty and short-term poverty. The problem is that any given pauper could have one of each of these pairs applied to him. Thus there were several general types of able-bodied poor to be considered, quite apart from any personal factors which might complicate any particular case. From a practical point of view the distinction of which overseers were most aware was that between mass and individual poverty. Underemployment was usually either a prelude to unemployment or a less severe version of the same problem and for the greater part of our period long-term, able-bodied poverty was relatively unusual.

The legislation of 1601 did not refer to any of these distinctions but provided a remedy which, with suitable modifications, could be used in all cases of able-bodied poverty. This was that the parish should raise a stock of materials on which the poor might be set to work.[1] Ideally such schemes were to be self-supporting, in that the profits earned by the sale of the poors' produce would serve to replenish and perhaps augment the initial stock. This policy echoed both popular concepts of charity and the normal methods of industrial organisation. When the parish issued an individual unemployed pauper with a stock of materials to be worked up and sold for the support of his family, it was acting in a manner not dissimilar from that envisaged for their trustees by charitable donors who bequeathed capital sums to be lent to promising but impecunious business men needing money to set them up in trade. On the other hand, when the parish made stocks available to the large numbers of workers thrown out of employment by a depression, it was merely taking over the putting-out function of their former capitalist employers.

The most serious obstacle a parish found in wishing to relieve its poor in this way was the difficulty of actually raising the capital sum needed to start. Since few parish records have survived from this period we know very little about how the parishes tackled this problem. The rates were better suited to paying running expenses than to raising capital but many parishes undoubtedly did raise an initial stock in this way. Others were more fortunate in that they received their stocks from a charitable gift or bequest. They could do this because the poor law had evolved out of charity and the two were not, in the early seventeenth century, as rigidly divided as they subsequently became.[2]

The greatest defect of the stock system was the tendency for

the capital to diminish with the passing years. There were
several reasons for this. One was the weakness of the administrative machinery. Spare-time overseers would rarely be able, let
alone willing, to devote as much time and skill to the supervising
of both the manufacturing and the commercial sides of the work
as would a private business man, nor would their labour force
be as efficient, since it was by definition that which the capitalists
had rejected. We can be sure that they would lay off their least
efficient workmen first, and that the parochial labour force would
consist of the least skilful workers and those who, though not
wholly incapacitated, were unable through age or infirmity to
make a living working on the normal terms. Furthermore,
parochial enterprise was always busiest when prices were low
and the demand small, since one of its main functions was to step
in and provide work for those whom the businessmen were laying off when production was reduced in the face of falling sales.
In short, it was too much to expect a venture run by amateurs
with an inferior work-force and operating chiefly in slump conditions to break even, let alone make a profit. The parish stock
might diminish or even disappear but the social benefits of saving
men and their families from the extremes of poverty and enabling
them to retain their self respect by continuing to work for their
living were not to be measured in monetary terms alone.

However great may have been the parish stock's contribution
to the relief of the unemployed during the seventeenth century,
it proved to be a blind alley as far as the long-term evolution of
relief methods was concerned. Many parishes must at some point
in the century have re-enacted the experience of Chiddingstone
(Kent) which first raised a stock in 1599 and replenished it from
the rates during the years 1603–5 but found that it continued to
dwindle until it was eventually used up on orthodox outdoor
relief.[3] This was no doubt acceptable in parishes where unemployment was not a serious problem and officers were glad to be
free of the additional duties which the administration of stock
imposed. Where the size of the problem obliged overseers to
deal constructively with unemployment, the trend even in the
early Stuart period was towards closer supervision of parish

work and the establishment of factories or even residential work-houses where the pauper-workers could be kept under constant watch. We have seen how the institutions which emerged in embryo during this period evolved until by the eighteenth century they had become the focal point of most schemes for setting the poor to work. The provision of manufacturing work for the outdoor poor tended to become a matter of supplying individuals with the equipment to set themselves up as craftsmen. This seems to have been needed more than the materials and the commonest example of this is the spinning wheel.[4] Many such gifts were, however, not to the able-bodied men but to widows and other women with a view to preventing or reducing their dependence on the rates. Parishes never forgot the possibility of providing work for the unemployed and we can find examples throughout our period, but generally the tendency was for the able-bodied to be brought within the mainstream of outdoor relief by being added to the pension list.[5]

It is not difficult to understand how this came about. We have already seen how several factors conspired to bring about the contraction of the parish stock so that if the stock was too small or non-existent the unemployed had to be relieved in cash. The same happened if the able-bodied poor were few and their condition likely to prove temporary so that there was no incentive to establish or to replenish a stock. Thus the forces leading to the depletion of the parish stock worked hand-in-hand with the motives of simplicity and convenience to persuade overseers to favour cash payments to their unemployed. Little harm came of this as long as the underlying causes of unemployment were not such as to create a continuing long-term problem and while the cash payments did not discourage their recipients from seeking work. These conditions applied in the majority of parishes for the greater part of our period and occasional doles or temporary pensions for the unemployed are a regular if not a frequent item in most overseers' accounts. The opportunities which work-houses offered for the imposition of work on the idle minority was a major reason for their establishment, but even where this was done authorities continued to realise that a temporary pension with a minimum of disturbance to house and home was the best way they could help the unemployed individual to survive and to find work quickly.

The workhouse was even less relevant in the case of mass unemployment which a slump could bring to towns or districts where a single manufacture, as often as not a branch of the textile industry, was the dominant employer. We have seen how the parish stock was raised and put to work and even embryo workhouses set up in response to the widespread incidence of this kind of poverty in the early seventeenth century. By the late eighteenth and early nineteenth centuries, when mass unemployment again became a serious problem, the cash pension had become the universal remedy.[6] It was recognised that there was little gain in setting people to work in those very crafts whose unprofitability had created their unemployment and the workhouses which it was economic to maintain under normal conditions were quite incapable of housing the vast numbers requiring relief during a depression. With poverty on this scale even the straightforward task of raising and distributing relief funds subjected both the human and the cash resources of the parish to enormous strains. Nevertheless the problem was temporary and the industry which created it also provided a sound financial base enabling debts incurred during a depression to be paid off during the ensuing period of prosperity.

Cash payments also tended to replace the provision of work as the normal method of relieving those whose poverty was caused by the combined effects of low wages and large families. In so far as the 1601 Act recognised this type of poverty, it saw it as a form of child poverty and empowered parishes to deal with it by taking the surplus children and setting them to work.[7] This provision applied as much to the children of the sick and widowed as to those able-bodied men and, so far as it was put into effect, it was a branch of the wider question of relief to children which has already been examined. Schemes for the employment of poor children were few in number and confined chiefly to the towns and elsewhere most poor families were relieved by pensions. When a case of poverty caused by low wages or an exceptionally

large family arose, there was every reason to relieve it in the
same simple, convenient way, but unless there was something
seriously wrong with local wage levels, such cases were rare and
their poverty marginal and as a result, it was often relieved in a
specialised way. If a family was entering a phase of low-wage
poverty, it would not feel an immediate need for relief but experience a reduction in its standard of living leading to the
elimination of inessentials, the postponement of occasional expenditure and a failure to accumulate savings for periodic out-
goings, of which the most important was rent. Thus large-family
poverty tended to manifest itself, not in a day-to-day failure to
make ends meet, but in an inability to meet certain infrequent
commitments. It was at this point that the parish was called in
to help. Thus we find that from at least the end of the seventeenth
century, overseers' accounts record payments of rents to people
otherwise not mentioned there. The numbers of such payments
steadily increased as the years went by. Of course we cannot say
what proportion of such payments went to supplement the earnings of widows, the partially disabled, and others, but there is
reason to believe that a significant proportion of the rents paid
by the parishes were for large families with low incomes. This conclusion is supported more by implication then by categorical statement. The cessation of rent payments was often specified in vestry
minutes as an essential element in economy drives or included in
the curtailment of outdoor relief in favour of the workhouse. It
is clear from mention in this context that rent relief was regarded
with less favour than pensions and its recipients as less deserving
than pensioners. Parish officers disliked paying rents, not only
because they objected to enriching property owners at parish
expense but because they were not free to distinguish between
deserving and undeserving. Furthermore there was always a tendency for the number of beneficiaries to increase, and the threat
of having a homeless family on their hands if they refused to pay.
The workhouse was the most popular solution to this dilemma,
but most parishes had no such institution and many realised that
forced removal to the workhouse was of no more long-term
benefit to the pauper or the parish than either paying the rent

or allowing the landlord to evict. Thus rent relief continued as
a thorn in the flesh of overseers. While there was reasonable
prosperity it did not get out of hand but, especially in the towns
where there were numerous families dependent on wages alone,
it constituted a constant threat to the precarious principle that
relief only went to those in genuine need, however caused.[8]

The provision of work, or the means to work, the payment of
cash doles, pensions or rent, these were the range of policies
which had been developed during nigh on 200 years as a means
of dealing with poverty among the able-bodied, whether its cause
was unemployment, low wages or a large family. These were
therefore the range of options of which overseers had experience
when the eighteenth century drew to a close, bringing with it
the Industrial Revolution, vast increases in population, and
problems of poverty among the able-bodied unprecedented both
in their magnitude and their complexity, for example mass cyclical unemployment.

Other industries created poverty peculiar to their own conditions. One such was the extraction of non-ferrous metals. This
was a highly speculative and precarious enterprise bedevilled by
geological and practical problems as well as fluctuating market
conditions. Therefore the demand for labour was irregular and
the payment of wages erratic. The parish was obliged to step in
to alleviate hardship and a tendency developed for families to
live on a chaotic mixture of relief and wages.[9] Technological
change could also create poverty. The mechanisation of a process
such as weaving[10] could, over a period of time, throw thousands
out of work, or at least make them uncompetitive. Men who had
enjoyed considerable prosperity by exercising their skills naturally
took time to adjust themselves to the new conditions, to learn
new trades and to find other employment. In the meantime their
old occupations could not support them even if they worked
excessive hours, and the parish had to come to their assistance.
Inevitably this was criticised on the grounds that relief would
serve to delay the search for alternative employment. There was
some weight in this, but it might equally be argued that the level
of relief granted assumed a working day of inhuman length.

The fact is that these were new problems and in their search for a solution the overseers' initial reaction was a crude extension of existing policies of cash relief, subject, if possible, to a work test. The poor law had been created to alleviate distress in a traditional society where life went on much the same from year to year. Changes were few and there was plenty of time to react and cope with new conditions, exploiting the opportunities and overcoming the problems which arose. But, with the onset of the Industrial Revolution frequent and substantial change was added to the problems facing parish officers. Naturally they adapted their existing relief methods to meet new needs. In the industrial areas where the new factories increased the rateable value they were reasonably successful; it was in the traditional agricultural sector that the old poor law met the problem which brought about its demise.

The Final Crisis[11]

In spite of the changes wrought by the Industrial Revolution, agriculture remained, in the early nineteenth century, the largest sector of the economy. This meant that when relief became mixed up with wages it could do so on a scale quite impossible in the other cases we have examined. Nevertheless, agriculture could not remain insulated from the changes taking place in industry and the story might have been very different had the Berkshire magistrates who met at Speenhamland in May 1795 lived in a wholly traditional society rather than one experiencing an industrial revolution.

Be that as it may, the crisis began with a visitation of the farmers' oldest enemy, crop failure. The harvest of 1794 was one-fifth below the average for the previous ten years and as a result the price of corn almost doubled. Wages had not risen in proportion and by the spring of 1795 there was extensive distress among the labouring classes.[12] It was to deal with a serious crisis, threatening mass starvation, that the Berkshire magistrates held their now notorious meeting. In effect they had to choose between two policies, either fixing an adequate minimum wage or paying subsidies to those whose earnings were inadequate. With the wisdom of hindsight they have been much criticised for choosing the latter. There is no doubt something in the argument that, as representatives of the employing classes, the magistrates were loth to raise wages which it might prove difficult to depress subsequently, but, since their decision is readily comprehensible in terms of poor relief tradition and the specific needs of the situation, it is unwise to lay too much emphasis on the concept of a deliberate conspiracy by the authorities against the poorer classes. There was the long tradition of poor law authorities making cash payments to able-bodied persons in employment, if their wages were too low to support their families or if their employers had to lay them off during a depression.

In the second half of the eighteenth century the rural parishes had evolved a peculiar method of making these cash payments which is of special relevance here. Mindful of their duty to set the poor to work, which, in such places, meant work on the land, and of their obligation to reduce relief if a man could contribute to his own support by even a little work, overseers had taken to dealing with those who applied for relief when they found themselves unemployed during the slack winter months by sending them round the employers of the parish to do whatever work they could find. They were then given relief enough to raise the total income to the level thought appropriate in each case. This practice became known as going the rounds and those who did it as roundsmen. The origins of the system have never been investigated systematically but it is the sort of theme which would merit research taking in all the areas where it was practised. We should learn a good deal about rural poor relief if we knew whether roundsmen appear, more or less simultaneously, in several parts of the country or whether the idea was conceived in certain localities and spread outwards, and if so by what routes. Without such information we do not know how widespread the roundsman system was in 1795. Wherever it was known it can only have served to strengthen the tradition of the parish augmenting inadequate wages in a manner especially liable to abuse by employers willing to secure their labour at wages subsidised by the parish.[13]

The crucial point was that all these wage subsidies were regarded as temporary, payable until a man found work, until his wages rose or his family responsibilities lessened or until seasonal or economic changes brought about improved employment prospects. The 1795 crisis fitted nicely into this tradition because there was every reason to believe that it, too, would be temporary. By Easter 1795, heavy winter frosts had ended hopes of a good harvest that year, but there was no reason to suspect that 1796 would be as abnormal as its two predecessors. When they gathered to deal with the crisis, the Berkshire magistrates would be aware that, however serious the problem may have seemed, in the normal course of events, it would not last for long.[14] After all, it was not the first such meeting to be held. In the past their colleagues elsewhere had met and dealt with similar temporary crises which were now part of history. As early as 1783 groups of Cambridgeshire magistrates were meeting to standardise the relief given to the unemployed within their divisions and in 1785 they responded to a deficient crop by ordering that all wages be brought up to 6s.[15] From then onwards scales were drawn up at divisional meetings from time to time and were in general use by 1800. Since this earliest example comes from the only county where the matter has been thoroughly investigated one wonders how many others may be awaiting discovery. The only other known pre-1795 example comes from Dorset where the magistrates issued a scale in 1792 in response to a local emergency, but two counties, Buckinghamshire and Oxfordshire, both adjacent to Berkshire issued scales at their Epiphany sessions, three months in advance of the better-known Speenhamland scale.[16] Other neighbouring counties followed suit, Hampshire in midsummer and Gloucestershire at Michaelmas.[17] Although in the present imperfect state of knowledge we cannot be sure that there were no others, we do know that, whether by magisterial authority or parochial initiative, the scale spread to much of southern England during the next few years.[18] It is clear, therefore, that the magistrates of Berkshire, in issuing their

notorious bread scale, were acting in accordance with tradition
and precedent. They followed the tradition that relief should
generally be given in cash to bring insufficient wages up to subsistence level in periods of temporary crisis, and the precedents
set by the magistrates of other counties in ordering such assistance, both in other crises and in the one with which they themselves were now confronted.

Indeed, the Speenhamland decision fitted so well into the
background of current practice that one wonders why it has
become so much better known than other similar decisions from
which it cannot be distinguished either by being first, or by being
especially significant for the future. The difference between the
Speenhamland and other scales seems to have been not in the
scale itself, but in the publicity it has received. As early as 1797
it was selected by Eden for publication in full and subsequent
writers have naturally tended to quote the example that was
readily available.[19] The 1832 Royal Commission did this, describing it in detail, but without implying that it was unique, since it
also quotes scales used in Sussex.[20] Thus, when later historians
came to discuss the scales, they found that both the fullest contemporary accounts of the old poor law featured the Speenhamland example, one giving its text, the other discussing its significance. It is therefore easy to understand how in thirty years
the Speenhamland example became converted into the Speenhamland myth. In 1854 Nicholls spoke of other counties copying
the Berkshire scale.[21] Subsequent historians were true to their
tradition of repeating one another and by 1927 the Webbs could
speak of the Berkshire justices taking the 'decisive action'.[22]
Almost all those investigating poor law relief since then have
relied on the work of these writers and so Speenhamland retained
its reputation as the crucial event down to the present day.

If Speenhamland was neither unique nor original in following
parochial and magisterial tradition and precedent, it remains
true to say that 1795 was a turning point in the history of the
old poor law. The watershed is made abundantly clear in the
overseers' accounts from rural parishes in the area affected.
Down to 1795 the pension list was brief and most of the names

were of females, chiefly widows. Children, invalids and old men
were in a minority and able-bodied men a rarity. Then quite
suddenly the list becomes much longer and the majority of new
names are male. Following the story through to later years we
find that this pattern remained right down to the end of the old
poor law. Herein lay the significance of 1795. It is not just that
the crisis was exceptionally severe, or that it was more widespread than its precursors—which seem to have been confined
to particular districts, but that it heralded a permanent change
in the pattern of poor relief.

The reasons for this are not far to seek. It is true that grain
prices eased in the late 1790s but before things were fully back
to normal they rose in 1801 to levels which made 1795 appear
to be a minor difficulty. Naturally the authorities dealt with the
new crisis in the same way as they had with its precursor of six
years before, using the rates to make up wages to a subsistence
level pegged to the price of bread. In the ensuing years prices
fell from their crisis levels but never reached those of the years
before 1795. The country had in fact encountered a phase in
which climatic and other changes regularly produced poor harvests and high prices. Some years were worse than others but it
was not until the 1820s that prices really became lower again.
Thus the temporary crisis of 1795 became a permanent crisis
and the temporary measures then adopted became a permanent
feature of poor relief.

Adaptability was the old poor law's greatest strength. It
achieved so much because it was free to devise new forms of
relief or adapt old ones to meet new needs and types of poverty
unknown in the early seventeenth century. But in this, its greatest
challenge, it was defeated and the way was opened up for its
demise. When the crisis of 1795 proved to be permanent the
defects in the bread scale policy became all too apparent. In the
first place it broke down the formerly clear-cut distinction between
pauperism and independence. Able-bodied men who at one time
might only have been forced to go to the parish in times of sickness now became regular recipients of relief. Once they had been
in receipt of regular relief under the bread scale they had no

H

inhibitions about seeking further aid when they felt the need, and indeed, as the bread scales became more firmly established, they came to regard such aid as their right. At the same time, employers found the bread scale system highly advantageous. Once the principle had been established that the parish should make up the difference between the wages paid and the sum needed to give subsistence at any given price level, they could keep wages low with a clear conscience and cut their costs by replacing independent labourers with those whom the parish was helping to support. In this way the whole labour force could be pressed into partial dependence on the parish, wages and relief could be irretrievably intertwined and part of the agricultural wages bill transferred to those ratepayers, cottagers, tradesmen and so on who employed no labour.

Other factors, some national, some local, tended to aggravate this situation as time went on. The most general was the increase in population which had begun well before 1795 and was probably a factor in the emergence of the roundsman system. There was much argument among contemporaries as to whether there was, in fact, a labour surplus in the agricultural south. Much no doubt depended on local conditions, methods of farming, land use and so on, but it does seem that, except for those places where agricultural methods were changing so as to expand employment opportunities, an increase in the number of people seeking a fixed number of jobs was an additional factor making for low wages. The end of the Napoleonic Wars in 1815 had a similar effect because the armed forces no longer offered an outlet for the unemployed and the return of demobilised troops must have increased the competition for work engendered by population growth. A further aggravation arose from changes in farming methods which positively reduced employment opportunities. The most significant of these was the spread of the threshing machine after 1815.[23] Agriculture, especially in its arable branch, is very much a seasonable occupation, but hand threshing was a slow process which could provide regular, if limited, employment for labourers during the slack winter season. The machines could do in a few days what had formerly taken as many months and with the poor law at hand to take over, farmers had no qualms about laying off their labourers as soon as the harvest was gathered in. In some areas the problem was complicated by changes in the fortunes of by-occupations. Most domestic crafts gave employment to the women, and sometimes to the men also, in the slack periods of the farming year. Textile working was ubiquitous and inevitably it suffered from competition with Lancashire, but there were also many specialities, usually involving work on a local product, which fluctuated in accordance with their own peculiar supply and demand patterns. Whereever these occupations declined the same results occurred. Men lost winter employment and the womens' contribution to the family budget was reduced or eliminated unless they could find work on the land, at wages so low that it paid employers to lay men off in their favour.[24] Thus the initial, but continuing, problem of high prices joined with the problems associated with population growth, the disbandment of the army, farm mechanisation and the decline of some domestic industries to create a general crisis of poverty among agricultural labourers which involved various combinations of male unemployment, female unemployment, under-employment and inadequate wages. The precise combination varied from place to place, for as in all aspects of poor relief it was the local manifestation of the problem and the local solution which mattered.

It is, however, easier to summarise the main factors leading to agricultural poverty than to work out how they affected a particular parish. Yet this is the task which confronts the local historian. We know a good deal about the general features of poor relief in this period from the welter of statistical material gathered by parliament. It is true that much of this is broken down to parish level and supported in a fair number of cases by detailed returns to the 1832 Commission and in a smaller number by the very subjective accounts which individual witnesses gave to the parliamentary committee of investigation. This material is useful because it gives opinions and precise facts which are not always clear from the mass of detailed administrative records. To make its fullest contribution however it must be used in conjunction with all other classes of local records in the kind of comprehensive inquiry into the social and economic structure of one parish which has already been described. In the context of such an investigation it should be possible to trace the ways in which high prices, population growth, mechanisation and declining industry contributed to the problem of poverty. We should also be able to assess its extent. How many people were involved, at different times of the year and in different years? How many were wholly unemployed, how many on rate-subsidised wages, and how many survived as independent labourers? Such a precise analysis of the problem would greatly facilitate our understanding of the expedients overseers adopted to cope with it. We should be able to see when it was all they could do to cope with the rising tide of poverty, when the task of raising enough money to keep the populace alive absorbed all their attention, and when they were seeking methods of making full use of the labourers they were supporting, or even trying to find ways to reduce the extent of dependence on the parish. There is much that we still do not understand about poor relief in this period and it is only through local investigations of this type that we can hope to extend our knowledge, since the abundance of printed material has meant that, if anything, the local records of what was actually happening in the parishes have been more neglected for this than for earlier periods.

We already know a good deal about the sort of thing the parishes were doing but we are ignorant of the ways in which the various policies were put together to make a coherent (or not so coherent!) whole. It seems fairly clear that the first two decades of the nineteenth century were dominated by the problem of high prices. The overseers' attention was concentrated upon the primary task of raising rates and paying out allowances in accordance with the local scales. Unemployment was relieved either by an increase in the weekly allowance or by the continuation of the old roundsman system. By the 1820s a rather different emphasis became apparent in the records. Prices were lower, so the scale allowance was less important, but the cumulative effects of the various factors making for structural and seasonal unemployment were making themselves felt more forcefully.[25]

The overwhelming impression created by the parish records is one of desperation as parishes lurched from one expedient to another in their search for a policy which would break the spiral by which the wage bill was increasingly transferred to the rates, or a way in which the cost of supporting the growing number of apparently surplus labourers might be reduced. Several expedients grew out of the old roundsman system. With greater numbers out of work it was possible for the parish to allocate them to employers who were expected to pay a proportion of wages which would be made up by the parish. In some places an attempt was made to push up the farmers' element by making employers compete for the labourers in a kind of auction. Later, a more sophisticated version developed, in the form of a labour rate.[26] This involved the parish levying a rate in the normal way but with the proviso that anyone would be excused payment in respect of any money he spent on wages paid to the unemployed. All these expedients had the same end in view. They sought to make relief dependent upon work, in the time-honoured tradition of the Elizabethan poor law, and to reduce the cost of relief by ensuring that all possible work was done for private employers before the parish stepped in. They all failed for the same reason that so many attempts to employ industrial workers during slumps had failed. It simply was not possible to give people profitable work in the very sector from which commercial employers were laying them off. Most rural villages were entirely dependent on agriculture and attempts to find work for the unemployed on the farms merely made the crisis worse by intertwining wages and relief even more closely together.

As a result many parishes dropped any pretence at profitable employment and concentrated on merely extracting some quantity of work in return for maintenance. For this purpose one task presented itself in every parish and in many it was the only one. This was road mending. Throughout the areas affected by the Speenhamland problem, gangs of unemployed were set to work to repair the highways. If some reports are to be believed they did not work either hard or long. It was difficult for the parish to enforce labour unless it was prepared to let wives and families starve, but other reports claim that never before had the notoriously impassable roads of southern England been in a better state of repair than in the early 1830s after several years of regular attention from pauper labourers. Road work was beneficial to transport even if its impact on poverty and poor relief was minimal.[27]

Another method of finding work was the artificial creation of opportunities within the agricultural sector by means of what was called spade husbandry. The essential feature was the reduction of farm work to its most primitive form by the elimination of all mechanical and animal sources of power and implements more sophisticated than the spade. Details of organisation varied from place to place. Very often a small plot was allocated to each pauper where he could grow food for his family. Elsewhere the labourers worked the land together to raise a cash crop the sale of which would raise money to reduce their dependence on the parish. The essential feature of whatever system was adopted was the creation of a crude subsistence agriculture, intended to help those thrown out of work by the market orientated one, the two systems existing side by side.[28]

During the final decade of the old poor law a more radical approach to the problem of rural poverty emerged. Earlier policies had been concerned with providing relief efficiently, preserving the connection between work and wages, and keeping the costs as low as possible. Nothing was done to tackle the underlying causes of the problem. By the 1820s it had become widely accepted, whether true or not, that in many parishes there were too many people trying to gain a living from a fixed source of income, in the form of the available agricultural land. There were two solutions to this problem. Either new forms of employment must be brought in or the surplus population must be removed to where there were opportunities for work. Nobody had any ideas as to how the former could be done except on a small scale in especially favoured localities, but there were great opportunities for the latter. The United States, Canada, South Africa and Australia had vast areas of land suitable for farming and the surplus labour of rural England had precisely the skills and experience required to exploit it. Of course, shipping people overseas was an expensive business and the willingness of many parishes to undertake this burden by means of loans or extra rates, is perhaps the best measure we have of the degree of desperation to which the Speenhamland problem had driven many parish authorities. They were prepared to lay out large capital sums as a kind of investment intended to produce returns in the form of lower rates far into the future. When one considers the speculative nature of such a venture and the ease with which a population might grow to fill the spaces left by emigrants one can begin to understand the feelings of parish officers after a whole generation under the unrelenting burden of agricultural poverty which they could neither understand nor overcome. We know very little about the numbers who emigrated at parish expense or whence they came. This is another of the poor law themes which would repay investigation without any geographical limitations, with the intention of tracing where and when the movement originated, the numbers involved, the details of its finance and organisation and whether there is any pattern as to the kind of parish which resorted to this expedient.[20]

Notes to this chapter are on pages 138–40

Conclusion

The past decade has seen a marked growth of interest in the study of poor law history, taking advantage of two major developments which have occurred since the appearance of the Webbs' comprehensive survey in 1927. First, there has been a number of pioneer studies which have investigated the potential of the various kinds of local records and shown how many of the problems raised by the poor law can be examined in greater depth. Second, there has been a vast improvement in the accessibility of local records. In most areas, the local record offices have now gathered the parochial documents, which must form the foundation of all poor law research, into central, properly equipped repositories, where they are readily available to all who wish to use them. The recent expansion in the quantity and improvement in the quality of work on the poor law shows that full advantage is being taken of these developments.

In the present state of knowledge three approaches are likely to be fruitful. The first is concerned with establishing the facts. In the course of this survey we have many times had reason to observe that we know what was done but not where it started, how widespread it was or what was the period of its rise, greatest popularity and ultimate disappearance. The medical contract, the growth of poor law unions of various types and the emergence of the roundsman system are but a few of the relief policies which we know were important, but whose precise incidence has yet to be worked out in a context of both time and space. It is essential that these basic questions of when and where be answered, since until they have been, it will not be possible to place a particular parish and its relief policies into a context which will show whether it was typical or not, an innovator or an imitator.

The second approach is concerned with the improvement and refinement of techniques for analysing the problem of poverty. These have been discussed in Chapter 3, but as yet we have little practical experience of them. They are, however, essential to our understanding of poor relief. Unless we understand the nature of poverty in a particular parish it is impossible to assess the significance of the policies adopted to relieve it. The first step is, therefore, to make use of these methods of investigation so as to improve and develop them until there is available to researchers a sophisticated and effective method of assessing the continuing problem of poverty in a particular parish.

Armed with the knowledge and experience to be derived from the first two types of investigation, the student will be better placed to engage in the third and most important. This is investigation of the poor law in the wider context of the whole range of human activities within a particular community or locality. People cannot compartmentalise their lives, and their experiences in business, church and politics must influence their thinking about poverty. Similarly, the vestry was not the only meeting place of the vestrymen both with one another and with the poor. They all knew at least some of the others through meetings in farm, factory, market place or residential neighbourhood. Thus poor relief can only be fully understood and, in return, make its fullest contribution to our understanding of the past, if it is seen as one among many relationships within a small community. It is however, a relationship which cannot be ignored, for how a community dealt with its less fortunate members must speak volumes about its underlying assumptions and attitudes.

Notes on the References
and Bibliography

The bibliography is an attempt to bring together details of a
substantial portion of the published work on poor relief. It is by
no means complete. Every effort has been made to trace all the
books and articles which deal exclusively with poor relief in the
period 1601–1834 but some have no doubt slipped the net and
others have been excluded because their content was trivial or
ephemeral. The line has to be drawn somewhere and it is inevitably an arbitrary one. In the case of work dealing with poor
relief in a wider context the bibliography is much more selective.
Again there is the problem of deciding when the treatment is
so sparse as not to justify inclusion. This kind of material is also
very difficult to trace. Much valuable work by local historians is
published locally and often privately and rarely finds its way to
other parts of the country. In the present bibliography most of
the works of this kind relate to Yorkshire and can be regarded
as a sample of what is available in other areas. A few theses
which have been useful are included but no attempt has been
made to list all those which are relevant.

Because most of the works cited in the references are included
in full in the bibliography it is possible to give abbreviated
references (author's name and date of publication) for these.
Indeed one of the functions of the references is to demonstrate
the enormous contribution which the published work, much of

it little read, has made to our knowledge of poor relief. The following abbreviations are used in the references:

BL   Bodleian Library
CRO   County Record Office
DA   *Transactions of the Devonshire Association for the Advancement of Science, Literature and Art*
DNB   *Dictionary of National Biography*
JEH   *Journal of Economic History*
JRO   Cumberland and Carlisle Joint Record Office
PLC   *Annual Reports of the Poor Law Commissioners*
PP   Parliamentary Papers
VCH   *Victoria County History*

References

Introduction (pages 9–13)

1 Eg Stokes, 1911; Grainger, 1915; Blease, 1909; Morris and Owen, 1918; Harris, 1926; Dodd, 1926
2 Marshall, 1926
3 Hampson, 1934
4 Eg Levy, 1943 and 1944–5; Coates, 1960–1; Blaug, 1963
5 Eg Rideout, 1929; Emmison, 1933; Hinton, 1940
6 Eg Huzel, 1969; Neuman, 1969; Slack, 1972; Taylor, 1969

Chapter 1: Policy and Supervision (pages 14–33)

1 Nicholls, 1854, gives the most detailed account
2 Eden, 1797, III, ccxl–cclxxvii and Webb, 1927, 443–5
3 39 Eliz I, c 3
4 43 Eliz I, c 2
5 Sixteenth-century poor relief legislation and the conditions which gave rise to it are discussed in Leonard, 1900, 22–131 and Webb, 1927, 44–59
6 Eg Northill and Eaton Socon, Beds (Emmison, 1931); various parishes in Essex (Emmison, 1953); Chiddingstone, Kent (Gibbons, 1959, 193); Edington, Steeple Ashton and Bishoptrow, Wilts (*VCH Wilts*, VIII, 12, 216 and 249); Norwich (Pound, 1962); Ipswich (Webb, 1966)
7 Eg Cambridgeshire (Hampson, 1934, 42)
8 This is described in detail in Leonard, 1900, 165–266
9 This was generally true in North Wales (Dodd, 1926, 112–13. One parish which has been investigated in detail is Ardwy Uwch Artro (Thomas, 1935, 155–6, 159)
10 Eg Wheatley, Oxon (BL MS DD Par Oxon) and Chiddingstone,

Kent (Gibbons, 1959, 194). The problems of an urban area, Cambridge, are described in Hampson, 1934, 26-8

11 This theme has been discussed in Leonard, 1900, 267-77 and Webb, 1927, 95-8. The ideas prevalent at the time are considered in James, 1930, Ch VI, and the local evidence has been considered in Howell, 1967, 314-19 and Beier, 1966

12 13 & 14 Car II, c 12

13 I James II, c 17

14 3 & 4 Will & Mary, c 18

15 8 & 9 Will III, c 30

16 35 Geo III, c 101

17 For a discussion of these see below, p 30

18 13 & 14 Car II, c 12

19 The records of these investigations are to be found in the Public Record Office, CO 391/10. John Locke's contribution has been published by his biographer, H. F. Bourne, *The Life of John Locke*, London, 1876, 377-90

20 See below, pp 53-4

21 A Commonwealth Ordinance of 1647 and 13 & 14 Car II, c 12, ss 4-14

22 7 & 8 Will III, c 32; for details of this Act and its implementation see Butcher, 1932

23 See below, pp 36, 81

24 9 Geo I, c 7

25 Ie Colneis and Carlford (Suffolk) in 1756; Blything, Bosmere and Claydon, Samford, Mutford and Lothingland, Wangford (all in Suffolk), Loddon and Clavering (Norfolk) in 1764; Loes and Wilford (Suffolk) in 1765. The operation of these unions is discussed in Webb, 1922, 121-38; Fearn, 1955 and 1958; and Lloyd Pritchard, 1965. One of the few rural local act unions outside East Anglia is discussed in Morris and Owen, 1918

26 22 Geo III, c 83

27 36 Geo III, c 23, see below, p 82

28 56 Geo III, c 46, see below, p 76

29 59 Geo III, c 12, s 1 see below, p 47

30 59 Geo III, c 12, s 7 see below, p 45

31 See note 19 above

32 PP, 1821, IV

33 PP, Old Series, IX

34 *Ibid*

35 PP, 1803-4, XIII

36 PP, 1818, XIX

37 PP, 1834, XXVII-XXXVIII. The report and its appendices

have been reprinted in the Irish University Press series and
some aspects of their contents have recently been discussed in
Blaug, 1964, and Marshall, 1968

38 For biographical details see *DNB*; L. Namier and J. Brooke,
    The House of Commons 1754-90, II (HMSO 1964), 499-501;
    Martin, 1972, 32-4; and Coats, 1960-1

39 For biographical details and bibliography see *DNB*

40 Eg Eden, 1797; Webbs, 1927; Marshall, 1926; Poynter, 1969;
    and Inglis, 1971

41 A recent example of such checking is Huzel, 1969. The need for
    it has been reiterated recently by Taylor (*JEH* 1969, 297)

42 Two editions with significant differences were published in 1725
    and 1732. Much information from this source was reproduced
    by Eden, 1797, I, 270-86

43 *A Legal Bibliography of the British Commonwealth of Nations*, I
    and II

44 The various aspects of county administration are described in the
    successive editions of R. Burn, *The Justice of the Peace and
    Parish Officer*. The records of Quarter Sessions are described
    in F. G. Emmison and I. Gray, *County Records*, London, 1948,
    and details of those which have been published are to be found
    in E. L. C. Mullins, *Texts and Calendars* (Royal Historical
    Society, 1958)

45 Eg south-west Lancashire (Oxley, 1966, 183-9)

46 See below, p 111

47 For details see *Guide to the Contents of the Public Record Office*
    (HMSO, 1963), 172-3

Chapter 2: The Parochial Executive (pages 34-50)

1 43 Eliz I, c 2, s 1

2 The legislation is discussed in Leonard, 1900, 67-73 and its
   operation in Emmison, 1931 (Northill and Eaton Socon, Beds)
   and 1953 (various Essex parishes); and Gibbons, 1959 (Chiddingstone, Kent)

3 For examples of these problems see Oxley, 1966, 30-2

4 13 & 14 Car II, c 12, s 21

5 Prominent examples are Norwich (Pound, 1962) and Ipswich
   (Webb, 1966)

6 Eg Cambridge and Wisbech (Hampson, 1934, 13-41, 59-65),
   Newcastle upon Tyne (Howell, 1967, 314-19)

7 Witness the numerous certificates most urban parishes were
   obliged to acquire from their neighbours, eg Winchester
   (Willis, 1967)

8   For local acts generally see above, pp 21–3
9   See below, pp 81–6
10 9 Geo I, c 7
11 22 Geo III, c 83
12 Published accounts do not always indicate clearly which system was in use in a particular case but Winchcombe (Glos) seems to have opened its doors to paupers from others on a contract basis (*VCH Glos*, VIII, 19, 44, 102, 172, 184, 206, 226, 228) as did St Andrew the Less in Cambridge (Stokes, 1911, 101) while the workhouse of St Benedict and St Peter at Arches, Lincoln, was founded on a combined basis (Hill, 1966, 157–8)
13 The terms of such agreements are to be found in Huddleston, 1962, 178; and Rideout, 1929, 106–7
14 For the formation and management of workhouse unions see Oxley, 1966, 292–5
15 31 Eliz I, c 18
16 Examples of this early activity have been described in Waters, 1933, 94 (Wakefield); Fox, 1953, 118 (Stratford-upon-Avon); Emmison, 1953 (Great Easton, Essex); and Raine, 1969
17 For some later, published examples, see Willis, 1967, 84
18 Accounts of such files have been given in Rideout, 1929, 63–87
19 Examples of work in this field are Pelham, 1937 and Rowe, 1953
20 Eg Wednesbury, Staffs (Ede, 1962, 173) and Patrington, east Yorks (Hopkin, 1968, 363)
21 43 Eliz I, c 2, s 1
22 Eg Harefield, Middx (*VCH Middx*, III, 252)
23 Eg Bingley, Yorks (Dodd, 1958, 58) and Forthampton, Glos (*VCH Glos*, VIII, 200)
24 Eg Elizabeth Swan of Monkwearmouth, Co Durham in 1734 (Kitts, 1909, 144); see also Oxley, 1966, 41–3
25 Examples of the divisions of labour have been found in Ardwy Uwch Artro where each overseer spent six months in turn collecting and disbursing (Thomas, 1935, 178); Chelmsford where each of four overseers served for three months (Ridehalgh, 1946, 203) and Trull, Somerset, where each of three collected the rate from a different part of the parish (Jones, 1952, 77)
26 Burn, 1764, 210–13, repeated most recently in Taylor, 1969, 95–6. The unusual aspects of the poor law with which Burn was familiar are recorded under the heading 'Poor' in his *Justice of the Peace and Parish Officer* (there are many editions but pages cited here are in the eleventh, published in 1769) III, 267–515
27 Poynter, 1969, 9–10 is one of the few writers to have remarked

specifically on this cyclical aspect of administration but it becomes apparent from reading many accounts of local administration, eg Erith, 1950 and Emmison, 1933

28 Many examples might be cited but Ecclesfield, West Riding, is interesting for having paid overseers as early as 1711 (Hey, 1968, 64), and Bourton-on-the-Water, Glos, for the unusual custom of employing a salaried overseer to serve in double harness with an annually elected overseer as his nominal partner (*VCH Glos*, VI, 44). The process by which paid overseers were introduced is especially well documented in Arwy Uwch Artro (Thomas, 1935, 179)

29 59 Geo III, c 12, s 7

30 PP, 1821 IV, 1822 V, 1823 V, 1824 VI, 1825 IV, 1826 III, 1826-7 XX, 1828 XXI, 1829 XXI, 1830 XXXI, 1830-1 XI, 1832 XLIV

31 The more important of these duties are discussed in greater detail in the following chapters

32 Useful discussions of overseers' records may also be found in Tate, 1946, 187-239

33 59 Geo III, c 12, s 1

34 See p 45 and n 30 above

35 Eg rating by the acre at Houghton Middleton and Arbury, Lancs, in 1744 (Oxley, 1966, 111); and by multiples of £4 13s 4d which had traditionally been assessed on the twenty-eight householders of Beckford, Glos, in 1704 (*VCH Glos*, VIII, 259)

36 Oxley, 1966, 111-13

37 Oxley, 1964, 17

38 Eg Blease, 1909, 138-47; H. N. Williams, *The Duty and Office of a Justice of the Peace* (London 1812), III, 664

39 As early as 1648 the mill owners of Wednesbury, along with the coal owners, had unsuccessfully sought exemption (Ede, 1962, 161)

40 The problem is discussed in M. Nolan, *A Treatise of the Laws for the Relief and Settlement of the Poor*, London, 1805, I, 136-8 and Williams *op cit*, 649-53. Local examples are given in Huddleston, 1962, 177 (Malton, Yorks, on the Derwent Navigation) and Oxley, 1966, 117 (Great Sankey, Lancs, on the Sankey Canal)

41 Various aspects of this problem are discussed in Nolan, *op cit*, 84-8; Burn, *op cit*, III, 479-80; Williams, *op cit*, 640-5; and Raistrick and Jennings, 1965, 297

42 59 Geo III, c 12, s 19, for a local example Blease, 1909, 165-71

43 Eg Tipton, Staffs, in 1604 and 1631 because of plague (Ede, 1962, 161)

44 For a general discussion and later examples, see Williams, *op cit*, 616–21

Chapter 3: Poverty and the Poor (pages 51–60)

1 For a general discussion of parish records, see Tate, 1946, 187–239
2 Webb, 1966, 122–40
3 Hudson, W. and Tingey, J. C. *The Records of the City of Norwich*, II, Norwich, 1910, 339–43; Pound, 1962, *passim*
4 Quarter sessions petitions and orderbooks have been used to good effect by Beier, 1966. See also Oxley, 1966, 183–9
5 Derbyshire was one county where this was usually done
6 3 Will & Mary, c 11, s 11; eg St Cross, Oxford (BL MS DD Par Oxon, St Cross b1 (d))
7 For a published example see Cowe, 1964, *passim*; Hampson, 1934, 178–9
8 8 & 9 Will III, c 30, s 2, and 50 Geo III, c 52, s 1. In St Mary, Cambridge (Stokes, 1911, 85) and West Ham, Essex (Sainsbury, 1966, 164–5) where the use of badges was enforced in 1682 and 1686 respectively. Examples of its occasional enforcement in the early eighteenth century can be found in Chalfont St Giles, Bucks (Edmonds, 1966, 7); St John the Baptist, Chester (Burne, 1965, 38); and Trull, Somerset (Jones, 1952, 91). Later examples can be found in Ecclesfield, west Yorks, 1775 (Hey, 1968, 66); Monkwearmouth, 1780 and Bishopwearmouth, 1788, both Co Durham (Kitts, 1909, 149–50); St Edwards, Cambridge, 1786 (Stokes, 1911, 86); and Cardiganshire, early nineteenth century (Davies, 1968, 19–20)
9 Thus the records of the one Cumberland parish of Dalston in JRO contains reports from four parishes: Dalston itself (SPC 44/1/5); Caldewgate in the parish of St Mary, Carlisle, in 1858; Castle Sowerby in 1836; and Penrith in 1818 (SPC 44/2/91)
10 8 & 9 Will III, c 30, s 2
11 JRO, SPC 44/2/91; a similarly worded request was appended to a list of paupers published by the Sunderland overseers in 1818 (Kitts, 1909, 138–9)
12 Eden, 1797, II, III, 693–904
13 PP, 1834, XXVIII–XXIX, eg 189–93, and XXXV–XXXVI, questions 15 and 25
14 For a discussion of these research methods see D. E. C. Eversley, P. Laslett and E. A. Wrigley, *An Introduction to Historical Demography*, London, 1966

I

Chapter 4: Outdoor Relief (pages 61–78)

1   Webb, 1927, 159–66
2   Some local studies have dealt with pensions, eg Edmonds, 1966,
    6–7 (Chalfont St Giles, Bucks); Ede, 1962, 168–9 (Wednes-
    bury, Staffs); and Jones, 1952, 90–1 (Trull, Somerset). Pen-
    sion Lists are printed in full in Cowe, 1964, 1–25; Oxley, 1955,
    193–4; Hampson, 1934, 177–9
3   There is some discussion of this point in Beier, 1966
4   Eg Todenham, Glos (*VCH Glos*, VI, 265)
5   This was the case in Westbury, Wilts, in 1801 (*VCH Wilts*, VIII,
    187); Sussex in 1801 (Caplan, 1969, *passim*); and the Shrop-
    shire parishes of Pontesbury in 1795 and 1800, Ford in 1800–1,
    Stapleton in 1790–5 and 1800–20 (*VCH Shropshire*, VIII,
    283, 234 and 167). In Norton Mandeville, Essex, the vestry
    was fixing the price at which pease and oats were to be sold
    to the poor as early as 1571–2 (Emmison, 1953, 25)
6   Examples of this ubiquitous practice can be found in Cutlack,
    1936, 38 and Peyton, 1933, 87 and 98. In Cardiganshire it was
    said to be especially prevalent because there were no work-
    houses (Davies, 1968, 17–18). Some of the problems raised
    by this form of relief are discussed in Oxley, 1966, 213–16
7   Buildings were erected as cottages for the poor in Cardiganshire
    (Davies, 1968, 16–17)
8   In Bottisham, Cambs, an old poor house and six cottages were
    converted into a workhouse in 1786 but they had reverted to
    their former state by 1798 (Hampson, 1934). Wednesbury,
    Staffs, converted the parish cottages into a workhouse in 1717
    (Ede, 1962, 164)
9   Examples have been found at Eaton Socon, Beds (Emmison,
    1933, 15)
10 Examples have been found at Lacock, Wilts (Hinton, 1940, 175)
    and Chalfont St Peter, Bucks (Edmonds, 1966, 11)
11 Examples have been found at Dolgellau (Ellis, 1929, 149); Brad-
    ford, Devon (Taylor, 1969, *DA*, 175)
12 Medical relief in general has been discussed in Levy, 1943 and
    1944–5 and Fessler, 1952
13 Early examples of doctors being employed come from Trull,
    Somerset, in 1674 (Jones, 1952, 93); Woodford, Essex (Erith,
    1950, 51); Gnosall, Staffs (Cutlack, 1936, 41)
14 Among places offering this form of relief were Chalfont St Peter,
    Bucks (Edmonds, 1966, 12); Bradford, Devon (Taylor, 1969,
    DA, 176); and the West Riding generally (Rose, 1965, 221)

15 Examples of contracts and their exclusions have been given by Nathan, 1957, 414–15 (West Coker, Somerset, 1778); Hart, 1965, 276 (Cheltenham, Glos, 1793); Kitts, 1909, 141 (Sunderland, 1783); Stokes, 1911, 104 (St Benedict's, Cambridge, 1832); Jeffries Jones, 1952, 225 (Abergwilly, Carm, 1805). The text of the contract used in Woodford, Essex in 1785 is given in Erith, 1950, 53–4

16 Eg Wednesbury, Staffs, in 1717 (Ede, 1962, 181)

17 Examples of parishes making this change are Trull, Somerset in 1785 (Jones, 1952, 93) and Woodford, Essex in 1775 (Erith, 1950, 52)

18 Contracts were rare in Cardiganshire (Davies, 1968, 21) and south-west Lancashire (Oxley, 1966, 226). In Frodesley, Salop, it was used for the two years 1828 and 1835 only (VCH Shropsire, VIII, 83)

19 For example, the Daffy bottles which make frequent appearance in the overseers' accounts of south Lancashire parishes can only be explained as containers for the cure-all Daffy's Elixir frequently advertised in the local press

20 The growth of the parochial midwifery service in Trull, Somerset, has been carefully documented. The first employment of a midwife was in 1627, the next in 1758, the third in 1771 and the practice became fairly common thereafter (Jones, 1952, 92)

21 Eg Bingley, Yorks, sent sick poor to Ilkley Wells in the eighteenth century (Dodd, 1958, 194); Cardiganshire poor were sent to Llanwrtid Wells in 1779 and 1833 (Davies, 1968, 22) and a pauper from Forden, Montgomery, was sent to Bath (Morris and Owen, 1918, 132)

22 Several parishes in Carmarthenshire sent paupers to sea bathe (Jeffries Jones, 1952, 226), as did one in Cardiganshire (Davies, 1968, 22), Patrington, east Yorks (Hopkin, 1968, 365), and Woodford, Essex (Erith, 1950, 56)

23 Waters, 1933, 62–3

24 The early history of infirmaries has been described in Brian Abel-Smith, The Hospitals, 1800–1948, 1964, 1–15 and F. N. L. Poynter, The Evolution of Hospitals in Great Britain, 1964, 43–71

25 Eg Bradford, Devon, subscribed to Exeter Infirmary (Taylor, 1969, DA, 176); Hasfield and Bourton-on-the-Water, Glos, to Gloucester Infirmary (VCH Glos, VIII, 288 and VI, 44); Bingley, Yorks, to Leeds Infirmary (Dodd, 1958, 94); Culham and Dorchester, Oxon, to the Radcliffe Infirmary, Oxford (VCH Oxon, VII, 34 and 52); Heston and Isleworth, Middx, to St George's, London (VCH Middx, III, 120); Norton, east

Yorks, to York Infirmary (Huddleston, 1962, 179); Almond-
bury, near Huddersfield, west Yorks, sent a patient to St
Thomas's, London for his lameness to be cured (Waters, 1933,
63) and in 1746 Chalfont St Giles, Bucks, sent a man to London to be cut for the stone (Edmonds, 1966, 13)

26 In the muniment room at the infirmary

27 Among dispensaries used by overseers were Aberystwyth, Cardiganshire (Davies, 1968, 22); Liverpool, Ormskirk, Warrington and Wigan, Lancs (Oxley, 1966, 239–40)

28 There is the example of a lunatic of St Botolph's, Cambridge,
who was first sent by the parish to his brother, then transferred to the workhouse, and finally sent to Bethlehem Hospital
(Stokes, 1911, 105)

29 For lunatics in workhouses see Kathleen Jones, *Law, Lunacy and
Conscience, 1744–1845*, 17–22 and 100–2; Walton, 1948 (ten
chained lunatics at Sheffield in 1791); Stokes, 1911 (St Ed-
ward's, Cambridge, built a special secure room in the workhouse yard for a lunatic in 1799). In Cardiganshire dangerous
lunatics were sent to the House of Correction (Davies, 1968,
23)

30 For parishes using private madhouses see Jones, *op cit*, 31–40,
102–7, 135–41; W. L. Parry Jones, *The Trade in Lunacy*,
1972; Oxley, 1955, 195 (Barking, Essex); and Erith, 1950, 56
(Woodford, Essex)

31 For examples of parishes using Bethlehem see *VCH Oxon*, VII,
52 (Dorchester); Erith, 1950, 56 (Woodford, Essex); and
Hinton, 1940, 178 (Lacock, Wilts)

32 Eg the description of lunatics in Liverpool Workhouse by James
Curry, *Medical Reports on the Effects of Water*, App II, 28

33 Jones, *op cit*, 49–51, 57–65, 83–98, 112–16; Samuel Tuke, *Description of the Retreat*, first published in 1813, reprinted in 1964
with an introduction by Richard Hunter and Ida Macalpine;
Norton, east Yorks, made use of York Asylum in 1826–7
(Huddleston, 1962, 179)

34 Jones, *op cit*, 51–7. For local examples see Oxley, 1966, 244–6

35 48 Geo III, c 96. For the background to this Act, its content and
implementation, see Jones, *op cit*, 66–78, 98–100, 116–26. For
a local example see A. Bailey, 'An Account of the Founding
of the First Gloucestershire County Asylum, now Horton
Road Hospital, Gloucester, 1792–1823', *Transactions of the
Bristol and Gloucestershire Archaeological Society*, 1972, 178–
91

36 Jones, *op cit*, 116 and 149 lists nine opened by 1827 and eight
more opened 1828–42

37 The ledgers of the County Asylum at Lancaster (Lancashire Record Office QAN/1/35/2–4) show that paupers were sent from far and near. They have been analysed with respect to the parishes in south-west Lancs in Oxley, 1966, 246–8

38 For epidemics in general see C. Creighton, *A History of Epidemics*, Cambridge, 1891

39 For the nature and incidence of plague see J. F. D. Shrewsbury, *A History of Bubonic Plague in the British Isles*, Cambridge, 1971

40 For local examples of how plague was dealt with see Fessler, 1952; R. S. France, 'History of Plague in Lancashire', *Transactions of the Historic Society for Lancashire and Cheshire*, 1938, 1–175; Leonard, 1900, 200–2. Sixteenth-century examples can be found in Webb, 1966, 110–18 and MacCaffrey, 1958, 115

41 Local examples are Dorchester and Tetsworth, Oxon (*VCH Oxon*, VII, 52 and 155); Woodford, Essex—hired and purpose-built pest houses (Erith, 1950, 51–5); Chalfont St Giles, Bucks (Edmonds, 1966, 13–14)

42 Among parishes which inoculated or vaccinated regularly were Trull, Somerset, 1771–1824 (Jones, 1952, 94); Dorchester, Oxon, 1780–1812 (*VCH Oxon*, VII, 52); and Woodford, Essex, 1801–29 (Erith, 1950, 55); Forden Union, Montgomery (Morris and Owen, 1918, 126)

43 Efforts to deal with typhoid and cholera have been described in Oxley, 1966, 252–4 (south-west Lancs) and Jeffries Jones, 1952, 226 (Carmarthenshire)

44 The problems of poor children have received attention in Pinchbeck, 1956–7

45 This was the policy in Oswestry, Salop (Goodman, 1960, 329) and Bradford, Devon (Taylor, 1969, *DA*, 171–2)

46 How overseers dealt with bastardy has been described by Oxley, 1955, 102–3 (Barking, Essex) and Cutlack, 1936, 62–3, 121–4, who also gives the texts of the relevant documents (Gnosall, Staffs)

47 An early example of setting poor children to work comes from Eaton Socon, Beds (Emmison, 1931, 111). A later one is the spinning school at Lincoln (Hill, 1966, 159–60)

48 See below, pp 79–101

49 Apprenticeship policy in particular parishes has been described by Oxley, 1955, 103–7 (Barking, Essex) and Goodman, 1960, 333 (Oswestry, Salop)

50 The texts of the relevant documents are given by Cutlack, 1936, 116–20, and Summers, 1916, 147–52

51 Published lists and analyses of indentures show that geographical location was the main factor in determining the occupations of apprentices. In rural Somerset all but two of the 170 apprentices put out by Trull (1618–1809) went to husbandry or housewifery (Jones, 1952, 97). Things were a little easier in Gnosall, Staffs, where 157 of the 178 children bound within the parish (1691–1816) went into these occupations while all but three of those bound out of the parish avoided them (Cutlack, 1936, 53–4). Another Staffordshire parish, Wednesbury, was nearer the centre of its industrial zone and could take advantage of the variety of occupations to be found there —coal-mining, gunsmithing and the various branches of metal working (Ede, 1962, 175–6). Rural parishes on the fringe of industrial areas like North Meols (Rideout, 1929, 100–4) and Great Sankey (Dunlop, 1932, 114–16) reveal a mixed choice of occupations

52 Evidence of a rota has come from Wakefield, west Yorks, 1600–50 (Waters, 1933, 64–5) and Trull, Somerset, 1716–1814 (Jones, 1952, 98). A ballot was used in Wednesbury, Staffs, late seventeenth century (Ede, 1962, 175–6)

53 Among parishes sending children to Lancashire mills were Wednesbury, Staffs, mill not identified (Ede, 1962, 176); Bingley, west Yorks, to Clitheroe (Dodd, 1958, 95–6); Lincoln to Bolton (Hill, 1966, 209); and Chelmsford, Essex, to Pendleton (Emmison, 1944, 77–87). Woodford, also in Essex, sent some of its children to a silk mill at nearby Waltham Cross, not as apprentices but on a contract basis. It also sent apprentices to a mill at Cuckney, Notts, and Erith concludes that they may have been better off going thus, in a group, than as individuals to masters in the east end of London (Erith, 1950, 71–2). Hanwell, Middx, also had an arrangement with a Cuckney mill but made little use of it (*VCH Middx*, III, 229)

54 42 Geo III, c 46 (1802, register) and 56 Geo III, c 139 (1816, scrutiny)

55 Exeptional examples of education for the outdoor poor has been recorded in Ecclesfield, west Yorks—the purchase of books (Hey, 1968, 65) and Llandereilog, Carm (Jeffries Jones, 1952, 229).

Chapter 5: *Institutional Relief* (*pages 79–101*)

1 Workhouses in general are discussed in Grey, 1972, and Taylor, 1972

2 Leonard, 1900, 225–7; Stokes, 1911, 87–94; Taverner, 1968, 67

3 Eg Manchester (Redford, 1939, 174–5); Stapleton, Salop (*VCH Shropshire*, VIII, 167); Wakefield, Yorks (Waters, 1933, 59)

4 For this Act and its implementation see Butcher, 1932

5 The record of these unsuccessful applications can be traced in the House of Commons Journals

6 This was certainly the case in Hull (*VCH Yorks, East Riding*, I, 164)

7 Eg Barking, Essex (Oxley, 1955, 108); Bideford, Devon (Duncan, 1918, 536); Doncaster, west Yorks (Miller, c 1805, 151); Pitchford, Salop (*VCH Shropshire*, VIII, 123). For other home counties examples see Webb, 1927, 216–17

8 9 Geo I, c 7

9 36 Geo III, c 23

10 22 Geo III, c 83

11 For Gilbert's activities generally see above p 28

12 These returns are discussed generally above. They have also been discussed by Grey (1972, 73) who gives evidence of an error in the returns and by Taylor (1972, 58–64), who states (pp 58 and 61) incorrectly, that the 1776 returns excluded local act workhouses. A spot check reveals the presence of Bristol, the best known of them all, Hull and some of the East Anglian unions which actually report their local acts in a marginal note. In this context it should also be mentioned that Liverpool was not a local act parish. For its workhouse see Oxley, 1966, 434–5

13 For an example see Oxley, 1966, 429, 435, 444 5

14 Published in 1725 and 1732 and extensively reproduced by Eden, 1797, I, 269–86

15 Stratford-upon-Avon (Fox, 1953, 119); Liverpool and Warrington (Oxley, 1966, 287, 422)

16 Eg Lincoln (Hill, 1966, 157–8); Bath (M. Nolan, *A Treatise of the Laws for the Relief and Settlement of the Poor*, 1805, II, 199–201), Southampton (Patterson, 1966, 55–6); Beverley (Hopkin, 1968, 216)

17 Eg Grimsby, Lincs (Gillett, 1970, 186) and Cheltenham, Glos (Hart, 1965, 278–9)

18 These various arrangements can be seen in the 1776 returns (PP Old Series 9, eg 316, Chester with all parishes in a union; 439, Oxford with most parishes in a union; and 468, Ipswich where each parish reported its own workhouse)

19 Eg Cheltenham, Glos, 1808 (Hart, 1965, 150); Tewkesbury, Glos, 1796 (*VCH Glos*, VIII, 150); Southampton, 1774 (Patterson, 1966, 56); St Andrew the Great, Cambridge, 1829 (Stokes,

1911, 98–9); St Andrew the Less, Cambridge, early nineteenth century (Stokes, 1911, 101)

20   The pattern and problems of rural workhouses in Cambridge-shire are discussed in Hampson, 1934, 92–101, 113–23 and in Oxfordshire by Oxley, 1964, 23–6, 50–6, respectively. The problems of individual parishes are considered in Emmison, 1933, 20–48 (Eaton Socon, Beds); Cutlack, 1936, 94–106 (Gnosall, Staffs); and Hinton, 1940, 193–8 (Lacock, Wilts)

21   Eg Rillington, East Riding, and Malton, North Riding (Huddle-ston, 1962, 178); Monkwearmouth, Durham (Kitts, 1909, 145–6); East Coker, Somerset (Nathan, 1957, 408); Hampton, Harmondsworth, Kingston, Hoxton and elsewhere, Middx (*VCH Middx*, III, 75, 229); Wellington, Salop (*VCH Shrop-shire*, VIII, 24); Winchcombe, Glos (*VCH Glos*, VIII, 19, 44, 102, 172, 184, 206, 226, 279, 288)

22   For south Lancashire and north Cheshire see Oxley, 1966, 425–58

23   The following are among the unions in the area for which exact foundation dates are known: Alstonefield, Staffs, c 1817 (White's *Directory of Staffs*, 1851, 742); Ashby-de-la-Zouch, Leics, 1814 (Guardians' Minutes, Leics CRO); Rugby, Warwickshire, 1818 (White's *Directory of Warwickshire*, 1875, 895); Claypole, Lincs, 1831 (Notts CRO, QDF); Appleby, Westmorland, c 1800 (PP 1803–4, XIII, 550)

24   These are discussed in Webb, 1922, 107–51; Fearn, 1955 and 1958, and Lloyd Pritchard, 1965. A rural local act union in another part of the country, Forden, Montgomeryshire, is discussed in Morris and Owen, 1918

25   Examples of both durable and temporary unions can be found in the list of south-west Lancashire Unions given in Oxley, 1966, 425–8

26   Listed in *PLC*, 9, 112

27   Eg Deal and Margate, Kent (PP 1834, XXVII, 218–19); Poole, Dorset (PP 1834, XXXV, 38); Lymington, Hants (*ibid*, 208); Reigate, Surrey (Eden, 1797, II, 719)

28   The workhouse test in various forms has been reported from Llangendeirne Carmarthenshire, 1797, 'except idiots and bed-ridden' (Jeffries Jones, 1952, 234); Wednesbury, Staffs, 1776, 'except sickness or any accident happens' (Ede, 1962, 167); Bottisham, Cambs, 1786, 'aged pensioners not disturbed' (Hampson, 1934, 113); Stanhope, Durham, 1830, 'partial workhouse test' (Raistrick and Jennings, 1965, 302); Chelten-ham, Glos, 1756, strict workhouse test rule not rigidly adhered to (Hart, 1965, 276); Southampton, 1753, except for temporary

relief and cases approved by the Workhouse Trustees (Patterson, 1960, 55)

29 Eden, 1797, II and III, eg 111–12

30 PP 1834, XXXV, question 15

31 Leonard, 1900, 225–7

32 Eg Mr Alcock's scheme of 1752 quoted in Eden, 1797, I, 311–14

33 Among the workhouse rules which have been published in transcription or summary are those for Milford, Hants, 1799 (Harris, 1926, 24–6); St John's, Chester, 1730 (Burne, 1965, 46–7); Easingwold, Yorks, 1828 (Cowling, nd, 119–21), and Southampton, 1753 (Patterson, 1960, 55–6)

34 We have descriptions of workhouse labour at Ecclesfield, west Yorks, (Hey, 1968, 65); Cheltenham (Hart, 1965, 276); Southampton (Patterson, 1960, 117); south-west Lancs (Oxley, 1966, 331–41)

35 Education was provided in the workhouses at: Chelmsford, 1790–1 (Ridehalgh, 1946, 206); Forden, Montgomery (Dodd, 1926, 124); Chichester, 1756 (Dangerfield et al, 1938, 150); Warrington, 1749 and 1836, Prescot, 1746 and 1769, and Liverpool, 1832—all Lancs (Oxley, 1966, 274–5)

36 Oxley, 1966, 269

37 Exceptions which have come to light are Handbridge, Cheshire and St John's, Chester (Burn, 1965, 45–6); Milford, Hants, 1799 (Harris, 1926, 26–7); Sutton near Macclesfield, Cheshire (Davies, 1961, 263); Easingwold, Yorks (Cowling, nd, 120); Southampton, early nineteenth century (Patterson, 1960, 117); Easebourn and Sutton Unions, Sussex (Caplan, 1969, 85–6)

38 Eden, 1797, II and III, 1–904

39 In this context it is worth noting that when the directors of Forden (Montgomery) Workhouse on two occasions reduced bread rations as a result of the bread shortage in 1795 they allowed extra meat and 'garden stuff' of the same weight (Morris and Owen, 1918, 100–1, 103)

40 Among purpose-built workhouses which have survived are those at Grimsby, Lincs—extension only, now cottages (Gillett, 1970, 186); Tewkesbury (a hospital 1964) (VCH Glos, VIII, 150); Thurgarton, Basford and Southwell, Notts (Caplan, 1970, plates 7 and 8); Bainbridge, north Yorks, in 1953 a county home of the aged (Hartley and Ingleby, 1963, 279); Harefield, private dwelling (VCH Middx, III, 252)

41 Among room-by-room inventories in print are those for the workhouses at Box, Wilts (Mellor, 1931, 346–9); St Botolph's, Cambridge (Stokes, 1911, 134–7); Milford, Hants (Harris,

1926, 21–2); Middle Division of Welshpool (Jones, 1903, 248–9)

42 Examples of converting other premises for use as workhouses have been found: in St Giles, Cambridge—six cottages, nineteenth century (Stokes, 1911, 113); St Clement's, Cambridge —a house, nineteenth century (Stokes, 1911, 106–7); Bideford, Devon—building purchased as almshouse, 1719 (Duncan, 536); Chichester, Sussex—almshouse which lost its endowment, 1681 (Dangerfield *et al*, 1938, 131–4); Gnosall, Staffs— barn belonging to the trustees of the parish lands, 1733 (Cutlack, 1936, 95–6); Lacock, Wilts, in 1758 and 1766 (Hinton, 1940, 194–5)

43 Among the many purpose-built workhouses which have been recorded were Corsley, Wilts, 1769 (*VCH Wilts*, VIII, 24); Sunderland (Kitts, 1909, 137); Bath (Nolan, *op cit*, II, 199– 201); Stratford-upon-Avon, 1780 (Fox, 1953, 119); Ecclesfield, Yorks (Hey, 1968, 63–4)

44 Committees were responsible for all or part of the workhouse management in Twickenham, 1740 and 1763 (*VCH Middx*, III, 156) and St John's, Chester, where, in the 1730s, the committee bought the food but a governor dealt with internal management (Burne, 1965, 44–7)

45 Examples of contracts come from Dorchester, Oxon, 1764 (*VCH Oxon*, VII, 52); Llangendeirne, Carm, 1799 (Jeffries Jones, 1952, 234); Harefield, 1825 (*VCH Middx*, III, 252); Monkwearmouth, *c* 1800, and Sunderland, 1797, Co Durham (Kitts, 1909, 148–9 and 141); Forthampton, 1795 (*VCH Glos*, VII, 206); All Saints and St Andrew the Great, Cambridge, early nineteenth century (Stokes, 1911, 95 and 99)

46 Salaried governors were employed in Woodford, Essex, 1796 and 1802–12 (Erith, 1950, 34–7); Cheltenham, Glos, 1755 (Hart, 1965, 275); Wednesbury, Staffs, 1781–1800 (Ede, 1962, 166); Warminster, 1757 (*VCH Wilts*, VIII, 130)

47 Oxley, 1966, 291

48 *Ibid*, 307–9

Chapter 6: *The Able-bodied Poor* (*pages 102–19*)

1   43 Eliz I, c 2, s 1

2   Among stocks raised through the rates were those of Stratfordupon-Avon (Fox, 1953, 119) and Ashchurch, Glos (*VCH Glos*, VII, 184)

3   Gibbons, 1959, 194–5

4   An example of both being provided comes from Twickenham,

Middx, where spinning wheels and flax were purchased in 1681 (*VCH Middx*, III, 155). A variety of tools, stock-in-trade and raw materials was provided at Eaton Socon, Beds (Emmison, 1933, 10); Lacock, Wilts (Hinton, 1940, 188); Dolgellau (Ellis, 1929, 150)

5   Eg Chalfont St Giles, Bucks, in 1741 (Edmonds, 1966, 19) although it should be noted that in the neighbouring parish of Chalfont St Peter stone-picking was required in return for relief (*ibid*, 20)

6   Bythell, 1969, 238–43

7   43 Eliz I, c 2, s 1

8   See above, pp 63–4 and n 6

9   C. J. Hunt, *The Lead Miners of the Northern Pennines*, Manchester (1970), 203–5; Raistrick and Jennings, 1965, 285–303

10 D. Bythell, 1969, 233–50; Oxley, 1969, 30–2; PP 1834 XXVIII, 277, 279, 909–10

11 Various aspects of Speenhamland, its origins, implementation and consequences have come in for considerable attention in recent years, eg Blaug, 1963 and 1964; Inglis, 1971, 44–54; Hobsbawm and Rude, 1969, 36–53; Marshall, 1968; Poynter, 1969; Huzel, 1969 and works cited below

12 W. Stern, 'The Bread Crisis in Britain, 1795–6', *Economica*, New Series, 31 no 122 (1964), 168–87

13 We have dates for the commencement of the roundsman system at Eaton Socon, Beds, in 1790 (Emmison, 1933, 51) and Bourton-in-the-Water in 1783 (*VCH Glos*, IV, 44)

14 For the background to this meeting see Neuman, 1969 and 1972

15 Hampson, 1934, 189–90

16 Webb, 1927, 177; Hammond, 1927, 139–40

17 Webb, 1927, 176–7, 179

18 Eg Cheltenham, Glos (Hart, 1965, 177–8); Yeovil division of Somerset (Nathan, 1957, 436); Cardiganshire (Davies, 1968, 24)

19 Eden, 1797, I, 576

20 PP 1834, XXVII, 68–71

21 Nicholls, 1854, 132

22 Webb, 1927, 177

23 For the introduction of the threshing machine, see N. Gash, 'Rural Unemployment, 1815–34', *Economic History Review*, 6 no 1 (1935–6), 90–3, and Hobsbawm and Rudé, 1969, 359–65

24 For a general discussion see Pinchbeck, 1930, and for a local example, Oxley, 1964, 73–4

25 For local investigations of Speenhamland and its implications see

Baines, 1961 and 1966 (Cholesbury and Hawbridge, Bucks); Caplan, 1969 (Sussex); Todd, 1956 (Sussex); Emmison, 1933, 50–64 (Eaton Socon, Beds)

26   The Royal Commission investigated these schemes in some detail and published their findings in their Appendix D, PP, 1834, XXXVIII

27   Among parishes where the poor were employed on the roads are Woodford, Essex (Erith, 1950, 46); Wheatley, Cuddesdon and Wigginton, Oxon (Oxley, 1964, 61); Lacock, Wilts (Hinton, 1940, 189)

28   For a general discussion see Barnett, 1967 and for local examples Whitehouse, 1970, 16–18 (Cottingham, east Yorks), and Erith, 1950, 49 (Woodford, Essex)

29   Examples of parish financed or assisted emigration are recorded in Corsley from 1828 onwards (*VCH Wilts*, VIII, 24); Stow-on-the-Wold and Bourton-on-the-Water, 1830–3 (*VCH Glos*, VI, 44 and 159); Dorchester, Hook Norton, Deddington, Stanton St John, Bicester, Oxon and King's Sutton, Northamptonshire, *c* 1830 (*VCH Oxon*, VII, 52 and Oxley, 1964, 75–80); various parishes in Carmarthenshire, 1818–32 (Jeffries Jones, 1952, 228); Norton, east Yorks, 1830 (Huddleston, 1962, 179); Grassington, north Yorks, 1830 and Alston, Cumberland, 1832 (Raistrick and Jennings, 1965, 303); Dolgellau, 1823–32 (Ellis, 1929, 153–4)

Bibliography of Writings on the Old Poor Law

Allen, A. F. 'An Early Poor Law Account (Shorne, Kent, 1590–1607)', *Archaeologia Cantiana*, 64 (1951), 74–84

Anon. 'Settlement Examination of Thomas Smith, 1766', *Notes and Queries for Somerset and Dorset*, 28 no 274 (Aug 1961), 33–5

Anon. 'Settlement and Removal in Bury', *Lancashire County Record Office Report* (1958), 14–21

✓Ashby, W. A. 'One Hundred Years of Poor Law Administration in a Warwickshire Village', P. Vinogradoff, ed, *Oxford Studies in Social and Legal History*, III (Oxford 1912)

Baines, A. H. J. 'The Vestry at Cholesbury, 1820–1894', *Records of Bucks*, 17 (1961), 57–71

——. 'The Select Vestry of Hawbridge', *Records of Bucks*, 18 (1966), 34–42

Barker, T. C., and Harris, J. R. *A Merseyside Town in the Industrial Revolution, St. Helens, 1750–1900*, (Liverpool 1954)

Barnes, S. J. *Walthamstow in the Eighteenth Century, Vestry Minutes, Churchwardens' and Overseers' Accounts, 1710–94*, Walthamstow Antiquarian Society *Publications*, 13, 14, 16 (1925–7)

✓Barnett, D. C. 'Allotments and the Problem of Rural Poverty, 1780–1840', E. L. Jones and G. E. Mingay, *Land, Labour and Population in the Industrial Revolution* (1969), 162–83

⩗Beier, A. L. 'Poor Relief in Warwickshire, 1630–66', *Past and Present*, 35 (1966), 77–100

Bevans-Evans, M. 'Local Government in Treuddyn, 1752–1821', *Flintshire Historical Society Publications*, 22 (1965–6), 25–39

Blagg, T. M. 'Newark Certificates of Settlement, 1697–1822', 'Willoughby-by-the-Wolds Certificates of Settlement', *Thoroton Society Record Series*, 11 (1945), 68–110

Blaug, M. 'The Myth of the Old Poor Law and the Making of the New', *Journal of Economic History*, 23 no 2 (1963), 151–84

——. 'The Poor Law Report Re-examined', *Journal of Economic History*, 24 no 2 (1964), 229–45

Blease, W. L. 'The Poor Law in Liverpool, 1681–1834', *Transactions of the Historic Society of Lancashire and Cheshire*, 61, new series 25 (1910), 97–182

Bond, M. F. 'Windsor's Experiment in Poor Relief', *Berkshire Archaeological Journal*, 48 (1944–5), 31–42

Bouch, C. M. L. 'The Book of the Overseers of the Poor in the Township of Great Strickland, Westmorland, 1778–1835', *Transactions of the Cumberland and Westmorland Archaeological Society*, new series 50 (1952), 164–70

Bouch, C. M. L. and Jones, G. P. *A Short Social and Economic History of the Lake Counties, 1500–1836* (Manchester 1961)

Bradbrooke, W. R. 'Fenny Stratford in the Seventeenth Century', *Records of Bucks*, 12 (1927), 6–23

Burn, R. *History of the Poor Laws with Observations* (1764)

⩗Burne, R. V. H. 'The Treatment of the Poor in the Eighteenth Century in Chester', *Journal of the Chester and North Wales Architectural, Archaeological and Historical Society*, 52 (1965), 33–48

▬ Butcher, E. (ed). *Bristol Corporation of the Poor, 1696–1834*, Bristol Record Society, 3 (1932)

Bythell, D. *The Hand-Loom Weavers* (Cambridge 1969)

Cannan, E. *A History of Local Rates* (1927)

Caplan, M. 'The Poor Law in Nottinghamshire, 1836–71', *Transactions of the Thoroton Society*, 74 (1970), 82–98

Caplan, N. 'Poor Law Administration in Sussex, 1801', *Sussex Notes and Queries*, 17 no 23 (1969), 82–8

Chambers, J. D. *Nottinghamshire in the Eighteenth Century* (1932)

Coats, A. W. 'Changing Attitudes to Labour in the Mid-Eighteenth Century', *Economic History Review*, 2nd series, 11 no 1 (1958–9), 35–51

——. 'Economic Thought and Poor Law Policy in the Eighteenth Century', *Economic History Review*, 2nd series, 13 no 1 (1960–1), 39–51

Collins, A. B. *Finchley Vestry Minutes, 1768–1840* (1957)

Cornford, B. 'Inventories of the Poor in Martham', *Norfolk Archaeology*, 35 no 7 (1970), 118–25

Cowe, F. M. *Wimbledon Vestry Minutes, 1736, 1743–88*, Surrey Record Society, 25 (1964)

Cowling, G. C. *The History of Easingwold and the Forest of Galtres* (Huddersfield nd)

Cutlack, S. A. 'Gnosall Records, 1679–1837', *Collections for the History of Staffordshire* (1936), 1–141

Dangerfield, M. E., Marshall, O, Stringer, E. R. and Welch, V. E. 'Chichester Workhouse', *Sussex Archaeological Collections*, 79 (1938), 131–67

Davies, A. E. 'Some Aspects of the Operation of the Old Poor Law in Cardiganshire, 1750–1834', *Ceredigion*, 6 no 1 (1968), 1–44

Davies, C. S. *A History of Macclesfield* (Manchester 1961)

Davies, M. 'Aspects of Parish Administration in Leamington Priors, 1823–1827', *Warwickshire History*, 2 no 1 (1972), 20–6

Dodd, A. H. 'The Old Poor Law in North Wales, *Archaeologia Cambrensis*, 81, 7th series no 6 (1926), 111–32

Dodd, E. E. *A Yorkshire Town through Nine Centuries* (Bingley 1958)

Downs, R. S. 'The Parish Church of High Wycombe', *Records of Bucks*, 8 no 1 (1898), 55–87

Duncan, A. G. 'Bideford Poor and Poorhouses, 1830–40', *Transactions of the Devonshire Association for the Advancement of Science, Literature and Art*, 50, 3rd series no 10 (1918), 533–60

Dunlop, G. A. 'Great Sankey Parish Papers', *Transactions of the*

Historic Society of Lancashire and Cheshire, 84 (1932), 91–125

Ede, J. F. *History of Wednesbury* (Wednesbury 1962)

Eden, F. M. *The State of the Poor* (1797)

Edmonds, G. C. 'Accounts of Eighteenth Century Overseers of the Poor of Chalfont St. Peter', *Records of Bucks,* 18 no 1 (1966), 3–23

Ellis, T. P. 'The Importance and Value of Local Records: the Dolgellau Parish Registers', *Y Cymmrodor,* 40 (1929), 131–83

Emmison, F. G. 'Poor Relief Accounts of Two Rural Parishes (Northill and Eaton Socon) in Bedfordshire', *Economic History Review,* 3 no 1 (1931), 102–16

——. 'The Relief of the Poor at Eaton Socon, 1706–1834', *Bedfordshire Historical Record Society Publications,* 15 (1933), 1–98

——. 'Essex Children Deported to a Lancashire Cotton Mill, 1799', *Essex Review,* 53 no 211 (1944), 77–81

——. 'The Care of the Poor in Elizabethan Essex', *Essex Review,* 62 no 248 (1953), 7–28

Erith, E. J. *Woodford, Essex, 1600–1836, A Study of Local Government in a Residential Parish,* single volume, 10, of Proceedings and Transactions of the Woodford and District Historical Society

Farmiloe, J. E. and Nixseaman, R. 'Elizabethan Churchwardens' Accounts', *Bedfordshire Historical Record Society Publications,* 33 (1953)

Fearn, H. 'The Apprenticeship of Pauper Children in the Incorporated Hundreds of Suffolk', *Proceedings of the Suffolk Institute of Archaeology,* 26 no 1 (1955), 85–97

——. 'The Financing of the Poor Law Incorporation for the Hundreds of Colneis and Carlford in the County of Suffolk, 1758–1820', *Proceedings of the Suffolk Institute of Archaeology,* 27 no 2 (1958), 96–111

Fessler, A. 'The Official Attitude towards the Sick Poor in Seventeenth Century Lancashire', *Transactions of the Historic Society for Lancashire and Cheshire,* 102 (1952), 85–113

Flinn, M. W. 'The Poor Employment Act of 1817', *Economic History Review,* 2nd series, 14 no 1 (1961–2), 82–92

Flynn-Hughes, C. 'Aspects of Old Poor Law Administration and Policy in Amlwch Parish', *Transactions of the Anglesey Antiquarian Society* (1945), 48–60

——. 'The Workhouses of Caernarvonshire', *Transactions of the Caernarvonshire Historical Society*, 7 (1946), 88–100

Fosbery, H. 'Notes from a Carshalton Vestry Book', *Surrey Archaeological Collections*, 26 (1913), 100–20

Fox, L. *The Borough Town of Stratford-upon-Avon* (Stratford 1953)

Gepp, E. 'Old Time Poor Relief Officials', *Essex Review*, 27 no 111 (1919), 115–19

Gerish, W. B. 'An Old Overseers' Book of Albury Parish, 1785–1804', *Transactions of the East Herts Archaeological Society*, 5 no 1 (1913), 16–20

Gibbons, J. 'Chiddingstone Early Poor Law Accounts', *Archaeologia Cantiana*, 73 (1959), 193–5

Gillett, E. *A History of Grimsby* (1970)

Goodacre, H. 'Ullesthorpe Overseers' Accounts', *Transactions of the Leicestershire Archaeological Society*, 18 no 2 (1934–5), 150–5

— Goodman, P. H. 'Eighteenth Century Poor Law Administration in the Parish of Oswestry', *Transactions of the Shropshire Archaeological Society*, 56 (1960), 328–42

— Grainger, F. 'Poor Relief in Cumberland in the Seventeenth and Eighteenth Centuries', *Transactions of the Cumberland and Westmorland Archaeological Society*, 15 (1915), 90–6

Gray, I. *Cheltenham Settlement Examinations 1815–26*, Bristol and Gloucestershire Archaeological Society Record Section, 7 (1969)

Grey, P. 'Parish Workhouses and Poorhouses', *The Local Historian*, 10 no 2 (1972), 70–5

Grounds, W. M. 'Old Billericay Workhouse', *Essex Journal*, 3 no 4 (1968), 218–22

Hales, J. 'Settlement Stories', *Norfolk Archaeology*, 35 no 1 (1970), 126–30

Hammond, J. L. and B. *The Village Labourer* (1927)

✓ Hampson, E. M. 'Settlement and Removal in Cambridgeshire,

K

1662–1834', *Cambridge Historical Journal*, 2 no 3 (1926–8), 273–89

——. *The Treatment of Poverty in Cambridgeshire, 1597–1834* (Cambridge 1934)

Hancock, T. W. 'Llanrhaiadr-yn-mochnant Vestry Minutes', *Montgomery Historical Collections*, 6 (1873), 334–6

Harris, V. D. 'Poorhouses in England with special reference to Milford Poorhouse and the Relief of the Poor in the Parish', *Milford-on-Sea Record Society*, 3 no 5 (1926), 5–31

Hart, G. *A History of Cheltenham* (Leicester 1965)

Hartley, M. and Ingilby, Joan. *Yorkshire Village* (1953)

Heelas, A. T. 'The Old Workhouse at Wokingham', *Berkshire Archaeological Journal*, 31 no 2 (1927), 165–72

Hey, D. *The Village of Ecclesfield* (Huddersfield 1968)

Hill, C. 'Puritans and the Poor', *Past and Present*, 2 (1952), 32–50

Hill, F. *Georgian Lincoln* (Cambridge 1966)

Hinton, F. H. 'Notes on the Records and Accounts of the Overseers of Chippenham (1691–1805)', *Wiltshire Archaeological and Natural History Magazine*, 46 no 159 (1934), 312–15

——. 'Notes on the Administration of the Relief of the Poor of Lacock, 1583–1834', *Wiltshire Archaeological and Natural History Magazine*, 49 no 173 (1940), 166–218

Hobsbawm, E. J. and Rudé, George. *Captain Swing* (1969)

Hopkin, N. D. 'The Old Poor Law and the New in East Yorkshire' (Leeds University Thesis 1968)

Hopkirk, M. 'The Administration of Poor Relief, 1604–1834, Illustrated from the Parochial Records of Danbury', *Essex Review*, 58 no 231 (1949), 113–21

Howell, R. *Newcastle-upon-Tyne in the Puritan Revolution* (Oxford 1967)

Huddleston, N. A. *History of Malton and Norton* (Scarborough 1962)

Hutchins, H. P. 'The Relief of the Poor in Chelmsford, 1821–29', *Essex Review*, 65 no 257 (1956), 42–56

Huzel, J. P. 'Malthus, the Poor Law and Population in Early Nineteenth Century England', *Economic History Review*, 2nd series, 22 no 3 (1969), 430–52

Inglis, B. *Poverty and the Industrial Revolution* (1971)

James, M. *Social Problems and Policy during the Puritan Revolution* (1930)

Jeffries Jones, T. I. 'Parish Vestries and the Problem of Poverty, 1783–1833 (Extracts from the Vestry Books of Carmarthenshire)', *Bulletin of the Board of Celtic Studies*, 14 no 3 (1952), 222–35

Jennings, H. R. 'Poor Law Administration in the Eighteenth Century from Poor Law Books', *Journal of the Royal Institution of Cornwall*, 22 no 75 (1928), 338–49

Johnson, H. J. M. *British Emigration Policy, 1815–1830* (Oxford 1972)

— Jones, I. F. 'Poor Law Administration, Seventeenth to Nineteenth Centuries, from Trull (Somerset) Overseers' Accounts', *Proceedings of the Somersetshire Archaeological Society*, 95 (1952), 72–105

Jones, T. S. 'Welshpool Parish Book', *Montgomery Historical Collections* (1903), 247–60

Kemmis, L. G. N. 'An early Thundridge Book of Accounts', *Transactions of the East Herts Archaeological Society*, 7 (1927), 222–7

Ketchley, C. P. 'Removal Orders', *Amateur Historian*, 5 no 4 (1961–3), 111–14

— Kiernan, V. 'Puritanism and the Poor', *Past and Present*, no 3 (1953), 45–54

Kitts, J. J. 'The Poor Laws, with special reference to the old workhouses', *Antiquities of Sunderland*, 10 (1909), 133–57

✓ Leonard, E. M. *The Early History of English Poor Relief* (Cambridge 1900)

Levy, H. 'Economic History of Sickness and Medical Benefit before the Puritan Revolution', *Economic History Review*, 13 no 1 (1943), 42–57, and 'Since the Puritan Revolution', *ibid*, 14 no 2 (1944–5), 135–60

Lloyd Pritchard, M. F. 'Early Days of Wangford Hundred Workhouse', *Proceedings of the Suffolk Institute of Archaeology*, 30 no 2 (1965), 175–82

Lucas, B. K. 'A Local Act for Social Insurance in the Eighteenth

Century', *Cambridge Law Journal*, 11 no 2 (1952), 191–7

Maccaffrey, W. T. *Exeter, 1540–1640* (Cambridge, Mass, 1958)

Marshall, D. *The English Poor in the Eighteenth Century* (1926)

——. 'The Old Poor Law', *Economic History Review*, 8 no 1 (1937), 38–47

Marshall, J. D. *Furness in the Industrial Revolution* (Barrow-in-Furness 1958)

——. 'The Nottinghamshire Reformers and their Contribution to the New Poor Law', *Economic History Review*, 2nd series, 13 no 3 (1960–1), 382–96

——. *The Old Poor Law, 1795–1834* (1968)

Martin, E. W. 'From Parish to Union: Poor Law Administration 1601–1865', E. W. Martin, ed, *Comparative Development in Social Welfare* (1972), 25–56

Mellor, A. S. 'Extracts from the Accounts of the Overseers of Box from November 26th 1727 to April 17th 1748', *Wiltshire Archaeological and Natural History Magazine*, 45 (1931), 342–9

Midwinter, E. C. *Social Administration in Lancashire 1830–60, Poor Law, Public Health and Police* (Manchester 1969)

Miller, E. *The History and Antiquities of Doncaster* (c 1805)

Mitchelson, N. *The Old Poor Law in East Yorkshire*, East Yorkshire Local History Society, 2 (1954)

Moir, E. *Local Government in Gloucestershire, 1775–1800*, Bristol and Gloucestershire Archaeological Society Records Section, 8 (1969)

Morris, J. G. and Owen, M. N. 'Forden Union during the Napoleonic Wars. 1795–1816', *Montgomery Historical Collections*, 37 no 2 (1918), 93–142

Nathan, M. *The Annals of West Coker* (Cambridge 1957)

Neate, A. R. *St. Marylebone Workhouse and Institution, 1730–65*, St Marylebone Society (1967)

Neuman, M. D. 'A Suggestion Regarding the Origin of the Speenhamland Plan', *English Historical Review*, 84 no 331 (1969), 317–22

——. 'Speenhamland in Berkshire', E. W. Martin, ed, *Comparative Development in Social Welfare* (1972), 85–127

Nicholls, G. *History of the English Poor Law* (1854)

Oldham, C. R. 'Oxfordshire Poor Law Papers', *Economic History Review*, 4 no 4 (1932–5), 470–4 (Pt I) and 5 no 1 (1934–5), 87–97 (Pt II)

Owen, G. D. 'The Poor Law System in Carmarthenshire during Eighteenth and Early Nineteenth Centuries', *Transactions of the Honourable Society of Cymmrodorion* (1941), 71–86

Oxley, G. W. 'Aspects of Poor Law Administration in Oxfordshire in the Eighteenth and Early Nineteenth Centuries' (Liverpool University Thesis 1964)

——. 'Poor Law Administration in S.W. Lancashire 1601–1837' (Liverpool University Thesis 1966)

——. 'The Permanent Poor in South West Lancashire under the Old Poor Law', J. R. Harris, ed, *Liverpool and Merseyside* (1969), 16–49

Oxley, J. E. *Barking Vestry Minutes* (Colchester 1955)

Patterson, A. T. *A History of Southampton, 1700–1914, Vol. I, An Oligarchy in Decline, 1700–1835* (Southampton 1960)

Peet, H. *Liverpool Vestry Minutes, 1681–1834*, 2 vols (Liverpool 1912)

Pelham, R. A. 'The Immigrant Population in Birmingham, 1686–1726', *Transactions and Proceedings of the Birmingham Archaeological Society*, 61 (1937), 45–80

Peyton, S. A. 'The Houses of Correction at Maidstone and Westminster', *English Historical Review*, 42 no 166 (1927), 251–61

——. *Kettering Vestry Minutes, 1797–1853*, Northamptonshire Record Society, 6 (1933)

Pinchbeck, I. *Women Workers and the Industrial Revolution* (1930)

——. 'The State and the Child in Sixteenth Century England', *British Journal of Sociology*, 7 no 4 (1956), 273–85 (Part I) and 8 no 1 (1957), 59–74 (Part II)

Pinchbeck, I. and Hewitt, M. *Children in English Society*, 2 vols (1969 and 1972)

Potts, W. *A History of Banbury* (Banbury 1958)

Pound, J. F. 'An Elizabethan Census of the Poor', *University of Birmingham Historical Journal*, 8 no 2 (1962), 135–61

Poynter, J. R. *Society and Pauperism* (1969)

Pugh, W. B. 'Agreement for Farming the Poor of Newtown, 1817', *Montgomery Historical Collections*, 26 no 1 (1892), 163

Purton, R. W. C. 'Leyton Poor Rate, 1674–1928', *Essex Review*, 60 no 238 (1951), 81–3

Raine, H. 'Christopher Fawsett against the Inmates: An Aspect of Poor Law Administration in the Early Seventeenth Century', *Surrey Archaeological Collections*, 66 (1969), 79–85

Raistrick A. and Jennings, B. *A History of Lead Mining in the Pennines* (1965)

Redford, A. and Russell, I. S. *The History of Local Government in Manchester* (1939)

Ridehalgh, J. 'Chelmsford Overseers' Accounts, 1790–1', *Essex Review*, 55 no 220 (1946), 203–6

Rideout, E. H. 'Poor Law Administration in North Meols in the Eighteenth Century', *Transactions of the Historic Society of Lancashire and Cheshire*, 81 (1929), 62–109

Rideout, E. H. and Dunlop, G. A. 'The Great Sankey Papers', *Transactions of the Historic Society of Lancashire and Cheshire*, 84 (1932), 91–125

Roberts, G. J. 'The Troubles of a Pauper', *Transactions of the Caernarvonshire Historical Society* (1949), 109–14

Rose, M. E. 'Poor Law Administration in the West Riding of Yorkshire, 1820–55' (Oxford University Thesis 1965)

———. *The English Poor Law, 1780–1930* (Newton Abbot 1971)

Rowe, J. 'The Laws of Settlement in Gulval Parish, 1739–1821', *Royal Cornwall Polytechnic Society Annual Report* (1953), no pagination

Ruggles, T. *History of the Poor, Their Rights, Duties and the Laws Respecting Them* (1793)

Sainsbury, F. 'Poor Law in West Ham, 1646–1836', *Essex Journal*, 3 (1966), 163–70

Salmon, E. F. 'Extracts from the Vestry Book of the Parish of New Shoreham, 1707–1779', *Sussex Archaeological Collections*, 51 (1908), 163–82

Sandall, T. 'Some Old Accounts of the Churchwardens and Overseers of the Poor of St. Mary's Parish, Stamford', *Re-

ports of the Rutland Archaeological and Natural History Society (1927), 16–23

Sheppard, F. W. H. *Local Government in St. Marylebone*, 1688–1835 (1958)

— Sinar, J. 'An Eighteenth Century Problem Family', *The Village*, 14 no 4 (1959), 140–2

Slack, P. 'Poverty and Problems in Salisbury, 1597–1666', P. Clark and P. Slack, *Crisis and Order in English Towns* (1972), 164–203

Smith, B. S. *History of Malvern* (Leicester 1964)

Steane, J. M. 'The Poor in Rothwell, 1790–1840', *Northamptonshire Past and Present*, 4 no 3 (1969)

Stokes, H. P. 'Cambridgeshire Parish Workhouses', *Proceedings of the Cambridgeshire Antiquarian Society*, 15 (1911), 70–123

Styles, P. 'The Evolution of the Law of Settlement', *The University of Birmingham Historical Journal*, 9 no 1 (1963), 33–63

Summers, H. H. C. 'The Poor, 1685–1734', *Collections Historical and Archaeological Relating to Montgomery and Its Borders*, 38 no 1 (1916), 147–52

Syers, R. *History of Everton* (Liverpool 1830)

Tapley-Soper, H. 'Non-Native Poor at Ugborough, 1587', *Devon and Cornwall Notes and Queries*, 14 pt 3 (1926), 134–8

Tate, W. E. *The Parish Chest* (Cambridge 1946)

Taverner, R. L. 'The Administrative Work of the Devon Justices in the Seventeenth Century', *Reports and Transactions of the Devonshire Association*, 100 (1968), 55–84

Taylor, G. *The Problem of Poverty* (1969)

Taylor, J. S. 'The Mythology of the Old Poor Law', *Journal of Economic History*, 29 no 2 (1969), 292–7

——. 'Poverty in a West Devon Parish (Bradford), in the last Years of the Old Poor Law', *Reports and Transactions of the Devonshire Association*, 101 (1969), 161–81

——. 'The Unreformed Workhouse, 1776–1834', E. W. Martin, ed, *Comparative Development in Social Welfare* (1972)

Thomas, Archdeacon. 'Merfod Parish Notes', *Montgomery Historical Collections*, 25 no 1 (1891), 6

Thomas, B. B. 'The Old Poor Law in Ardudwy-Uwch-Artro',

Bulletin of the Board of Celtic Studies, 7 no 2 (1935), 153–91

Thomas, G. B. 'Llanaber Vestry Records, 1724–54', *Journal of the Merioneth Historical Record Society*, 2 (1953–6), 271–84

Thomas, H. 'An Old Vestry Book (St. Cadfan, Towyn)', *Journal of the Merioneth Historical Record Society*, 2 (1953–6), 39–44

Thomas, W. K. 'Crabbe's Workhouse', *Huntingdon Library Quaterly*, 32 no 2 (1968), 149–61

Todd, A. C. 'An Answer to Poverty in Sussex, 1830–45', *Agricultural History Review*, 4 (1956), 45–51

Trotter, E. *Seventeenth Century Life in the Country Parish with Special Reference to Local Government* (Cambridge 1919)

Waite, H. E. 'Whitchurch Canonicorum Parish Vestry, 1772–1796', *Proceedings of the Dorset Natural History and Archaeological Society*, 76 (1954), 100–9

Walton, M. *Sheffield: Its Story and Its Achievements* (Sheffield 1948)

Waters, S. H. *Wakefield in the Seventeenth Century* (Wakefield 1933)

Webb, J. *Poor Relief in Elizabethan Ipswich*, Suffolk Record Society, 9 (1966)

Webb, S. and B. *Statutory Authorities for Special Purposes* (1922)
——. *English Poor Law History, Part 1, The Old Poor Law* (1927)

Whitehouse, J. *Cottingham's Care of Its Poor to 1834*, Cottingham (E Yorks) Local History Society (1970)

— Willis, A. J. *Winchester Settlement Papers, 1667–1842* (Folkestone 1967)

Wilson, M., Crighton, J. D., Johnson, E. I. and Barrett, P. *Pershore, A Short History* (Pershore 1972)

Acknowledgements

I have received generous assistance from many people: from the librarians and staffs of the University Libraries of Liverpool, Oxford, Leicester and Kingston upon Hull and the City Library of Kingston upon Hull, from colleagues in the various record offices I have had cause to visit, from Professor J. R. Harris who guided my first ventures into the history of poor relief and from Dr M. E. Rose who first suggested this book and offered valuable advice on its composition. The dedication reflects my debt of gratitude to my father who not only first introduced me to the poor law but also read the present text in all its stages and to my mother who converted a chaotic manuscript into an impeccable typescript. This book could never have been completed without the constant support and sympathy of my wife. The contributions of others have been many but any errors and omissions are my own.

G.W.O.

Index